THE WHOLE BEAST

 NOSE TO TAIL EATING

THE
WHOLE BEAST

FERGUS
HENDERSON

INTRODUCTION BY
ANTHONY BOURDAIN

An Imprint of HarperCollinsPublishers

For Margot and Annabelle

HarperCollins books may be purchased for educational, business, or sales
promotional use. For information, please e-mail the Special Markets
Department at SPsales@harpercollins.com.

FIRST EDITION

Designed by Jessica Shatan Heslin

Library of Congress Cataloging-in-Publication Data has been applied for.
ISBN: 0-06-058536-6

18 19 20 ❖/LSC 30 29 28 27 26 25

CONTENTS

STARTERS

(Smaller But Often Sustaining Dishes)

LAMB'S BRAINS AND SWEETBREADS

MEAT

BIRDS AND GAME

FISH AND SHELLFISH

VEGETABLES

DRESSINGS, SAUCES, AND PICKLES

PUDDINGS AND SAVORIES

BAKING

Acknowledgments

Thank you, Mum for your cooking, Dad for your generosity over the years of many splendid gastronomic moments, Charles Campbell for much inspiration, Jon Spiteri, Trevor Gulliver, and all at St. John, especially Dorothy Harrison.

INTRODUCTION

The book you hold in your hand has been considered, for too many years, to be a cult masterpiece, an obscure object of desire for chefs, food writers, cookbook collectors, and international foodies, yearned for, sought out, searched for by those who didn't own a copy, cherished and protected by those lucky few who did. Once available only in the United Kingdom, even there, copies seemed quickly to disappear. A few lucky chefs would return from their pilgrimages to The Restaurant, glassy-eyed, like new converts, smiling serenely. They wouldn't brag about their find. (They might then be asked to lend their copies.) They didn't show them around—as The Book might become damaged or smudged. Once in a great while, when a fellow chef, or intensely curious gourmet would raise the subject of St. John or Fergus Henderson and ask whether anyone present had eaten there, or seen The Book, some might let slip with quiet understatement, "Oh, yeah. I have a copy. I bought it at The Restaurant." This would usually be followed by a long moment of pained silence as others less fortunate ground their teeth and clenched their fists with envy.

Now, at long last, Fergus Henderson's magnificent, legendary *The Whole Beast: Nose to Tail Eating* is available in the United States—a historic document which when first published, flew in the face of accepted culinary doctrine, both as proud proclamation of the true glories of pork, offal, and the neglected bits of animals we love to eat, and a refutation of the once deeply held belief that the English couldn't and never could cook. The Restaurant, St. John, when it first opened in London's then off-the-beaten-path Smithfield district, had an electrifying effect on chefs who ate there—and this Book helped spread the word. You could make a good argument that Fergus Henderson's early and unpredictable success in a plain whitewashed room on St. John Street in London made it permissible for all of us—chefs as far away as New York, San Francisco, and Portland—to reconsider dishes and menu items that were once the very foundations of French, Italian and, yes—even American cuisine. Every time you see pork belly or bone marrow, kidneys or trotters (increasingly "hot" offerings) on an American menu—you might well owe a debt of thanks to Fergus, who showed so many of us the way—who allowed chefs who might otherwise have feared to do so to also go against the tide. Any time you see cheeks, tripes, or marrow on a New York City menu you can feel the ripples of his influence—and the special place he holds in the affections of his fellow chefs.

After eating the Roast Bone Marrow and Parsley Salad (page 35) at St. John, I declared it my always and forever choice for my "Death Row Meal," the last meal I'd choose to put in my mouth before they turned up the juice. Every subsequent experience at The Restaurant hit me like a percussion grenade—an eye-opening, inspiring, thoroughly pleasurable yet stripped-down adventure in dining—a nonsense-free exaltation of what's good—and has always been good—about food and cooking at its best. Like many of St. John's customers, I became immediately and annoyingly evangelical on the subject, attributing to Fergus all kinds of revolutionary/reactionary socio-political motives. My enthusiastic rant in my book *A Cook's Tour* made him sound like George Washington, Ho Chi Minh, Lord Nelson, Orson Welles, Pablo Picasso, and Abbie Hoffman—all rolled into one. I saw his simple, honest, traditional English country fare as a thumb in the eye to the establishment, an outrageously timed head butt to the growing hordes of the politically correct, the PETA people, the European Union, practitioners of arch, ironic Fusion Cuisine, and all those chefs who were fussing about with tall, overly sculpted entrees of little substance and less soul.

I'm sure I embarrassed him. Because, of course, Fergus Henderson is no bomb-throwing ideologue. I doubt very much if the words "cutting edge" ever occurred to him. I'm quite sure, now that I've come to know him, that he in no way saw the simple, lovely, unassuming, and unpretentious food in this book to be an insult or an affront to anyone—much less a statement of any kind. It is instead, I think, a reminder—and a respectful one at that—of what is good about food, about the essential, nearly forgotten elements of a great meal, an homage, an honoring of the foodstuffs we eat, a refutation only of waste and disregard. If *The Whole Beast*  makes a statement, it's that nearly every part of nearly everything we eat, in the hands of a patient and talented cook, can be delicious—something most good cooks and most French and Italian mothers have known for centuries. It honors the past at least as much as it points the way to a brave new future. This is fundamentally, though, a book about simple, good things.

Ask any chefs of any three-star Michelin restaurant what their favorite single dish to eat is—and you will often get an answer like "confit of duck" or "my mother's pied de cochon" or "a well-braised shank of lamb or veal." These were the dishes that first taught many of us to cook, the absolute foundation of haute cuisine. Nearly anyone—after a few tries—can grill a filet mignon or a sirloin steak. A trained chimp can steam a lobster. But it takes love, and time, and respect for one's ingredients to properly deal with a pig's ear or a kidney. And the rewards are enormous. The Crispy Pig's Tails (page 72) at St. John are some of the most delicious things you will ever put in your mouth. And while it's easy to associate St. John and Fergus with an atmosphere of unrestrained carnivorousness, he brings the same appreciation for every part of the ingredient to seafood: his Soft Roes on Toast (page 133), a simple presentation of a particular issue of herring, is destined to be—one day—the next big thing on New York menus, a "where have you been my whole life" appetizer.

St. John has quickly become a must-try on the international traveling chef circuit. Chefs, foodies, food writers, and cooks on sabbatical, traveling perhaps through the great multistarred restaurants of London, France, and Spain often stop there for a taste of the real, to find out what all the buzz is about. Who *is* this Fergus Henderson? *Why* do people who visit his restaurant and eat his food return with glazed, blissful, and strangely knowing looks on their faces? I remember with pleasure, a few years ago, walking into a hot restaurant on New York's Lower East Side and seeing Fergus's Roast Bone Marrow and Parsley Salad reproduced, note for note, on the menu—and the comforting sense of recognition that I had a soul mate in their kitchen—that the chef—whoever she was—was "one of us," somebody who'd "been," someone hip to the restaurant that so many of us would love to run—but for various reasons, just can't. Scared? Intimidated? Grossed out? Put off by sense memories of Mom, or some long-ago lunch lady coming at you with a slab of ineptly and indifferently fried liver, or some comedian's jokes about haggis? Does the phrase *Eat it*! It's good for you!" still strike fear in your heart? Consider the following incident, at a recent special meal held at Portland's Heathman Restaurant. The menu, in my honor, consisted entirely of offal and nasty bits: kidneys, livers, cock's combs, headcheese, and sweetbreads. The crowd coming in bore expressions ranging from apprehensive to hopeful. It was the older customers who looked the most optimistic. They remembered the early days of American menus, when ox hearts and tripes bore no mysteries, and they recalled those things with pleasure. Southerners, who had never forgotten chitterlings and pig's feet and hog maws, seemed almost misty-eyed. And culinary novices— young cooks, heavily pierced and tattooed metalheads, thin, well-dressed adventuresses, practitioners of "extreme" eating who saw the night's fare, perhaps, as an extension of "extreme" sports, all came looking excited but uncertain. To see the expressions on their faces—after a few bites of rabbit kidney or sweetbread—was a beautiful thing. A moment of recognition, a calming, reassuring wave of satisfaction, the dawning knowledge that yes—this can be good. I like it. I love it. I want it again.

Of course, it's not all hooves and snouts and guts. Lamb and Barley Stew (page 93), Roast Woodcock (page 107), Mutton and Beans (page 102), Jugged Hare (page 123), Kedgeree (page 131), and Boiled Ham and Parsley Sauce (page 66) are about as English and as unthreatening as you can get; simple, nourishing, beautiful to gaze upon; country cooking at its very finest. Skate, Capers, and Bread (page145) and Deviled Crab (page 130) should not frighten—only delight—even the most conservative eaters—and will hopefully lure them into deeper waters. Warm Pig's Head (page 30) should make a convert of anyone who thought they'd never eat any dish with "head" in its name—a dish so wonderful, so Goddamn amazing that it borders on religious epiphany.

Fergus Henderson is a quiet, modest man, prone to dry statements—as when contemplating a roast suckling pig. "This was a noble animal. A happy pig." But he inspires hyperbole in others. First-time visitors to St. John frequently come away transformed—and raving about the experience. A trip to the bare, abattoir-like space becomes a voyage of discovery—or more accurately of re-discovery; of long forgotten childhoods—or childhoods we never had but somehow had always yearned for. It is my favorite restaurant in the world—and I suspect a lot of people share my devotion. Hopefully, these pages will be the start of your own voyage. Welcome to the club.

—ANTHONY BOURDAIN

SEVEN THINGS
I SHOULD MENTION

1. *The Whole Beast: Nose to Tail Eating*

This is a celebration of cuts of meat, innards, and extremities that are more often forgotten or discarded in today's kitchen; it would seem disingenuous to the animal not to make the most of the whole beast: there is a set of delights, textural and flavorsome, which lie beyond the fillet.

2. Vegetables, Seasons, and Condiments

Given the carnivorous overtones of a book on the whole beast, it is possible to forget the holistic (not wanting to sound New Age) connotations of "nose to tail eating." There is equal respect for the carrot; once radishes are eaten, their leaves are turned into a peppery salad. The spirit of time and place, enjoying the limitations of the indigenous seasons. Having sourced happy ingredients it only seems appropriate that we make our own condiments to accompany them. Be it ketchup, celery salt, or chutney, they all make up the whole beast, "nose to tail eating."

3. Time and Preserving

Taking time with your food does not mean long intricate recipes, just a little thinking ahead; an ox tongue in brine (a salt and sugar solution), or a bucket of cabbage salting in the corner of your kitchen, what could be more reassuring? Out of the traditional methods of preserving, delicious results are to be found for stocking your cupboard for leaner months: salting, drying, pickling, curing, potting, and preserving in fat. Again, not long and complicated processes, just a matter of time, which contrary to today's mood, we still have on our side.

4. Bones

There is nothing finer than having a bone to gnaw on at the end of meal; meat will cook better on the bone; and your stockpot appreciates the contribution of plenty of bones. Our signature dish at St. John is Roast Bone Marrow and Parsley Salad (the marrow comes from the middle of veal leg bones), a dish that encompasses many of my foodie beliefs, such as the eater being encouraged to bring a set of ingredients together at the table—there is hands-on grappling with bones, last-minute seasoning with coarse sea salt is required, so the food coming out of the kitchen is not a *fait accompli*, but the process continues at the table.

5. Lunch at Sweetings

There is much to be learned from a lunch at Sweetings, a fish restaurant in the City of London. You sit at a bar behind which a waiter is trapped, you order your smoked eel, they yell to a runner who delivers your eel over your shoulder to the incarcerated waiter, who then places it under the counter and then in front of you as if they had had it all along. Not an entirely practical way of getting your food, but a splendid ritual and a reminder that a wonderful lunch can come in many ways.

6. Cooking at Home, Don't Be Afraid

This is a book about cooking and eating at home with friends and relations, not replicating restaurant plates of food. Do not be afraid of cooking, as your ingredients will know and misbehave. Enjoy your cooking and the food will behave; moreover it will pass your pleasure on to those who eat it.

7. Coming to America

I have heard it said that our food is too extreme for America, our use of the whole beast. My experience is that every time someone comes to the kitchen at St. John to say how much they enjoyed our Pig's Head or Rolled Spleen, they are always American, so I have no doubt that the strong gastronomic spirit of adventure in the United States will carry them through the recipes in the book. As to the availability of any of the cuts of meat, beasts are beasts; some have longer horns and others shorter tails, but they are basically made up of the same parts. I recommend developing a good relationship with your butcher, who will know how to find comparable cuts; in fact I'm not sure there is any better bit of advice to end on.

STOCKS

Basic Stocks

Essentials

Stock is fundamental, but it's also easy. All you have to do is remember to keep your bones, giblets, and shells. There is almost nothing as reassuring as having some stock up your sleeve.

Stock vegetables can be defined by what you have on hand, though you should not be too cavalier in your approach to stock, and it does not take too much trouble to have the right vegetables: onions (with skin on, chopped in half); a head of garlic (with skin on, chopped in half); carrots (peeled and split lengthwise); a leek (split lengthwise and cleaned); fennel; celery and its leaf; red onions if you want a darker stock (skin on and cut in half); mushroom peelings if you have some on hand; a bay leaf; herbs, or simply the stems of parsley; peppercorns: please feel free to express yourself.

The other essential ingredient is water; you want to cover your stock ingredients with enough to allow for skimming (which is vital), but not so much as to drown any possible flavor. Bring to a simmer, but not a rolling boil, as this will boil the surface scum back into the stock. I shall again say *skim*. To know when a stock is ready, taste and taste again, though the timings given below should be a good guide. Have the bones and vegetables released their goodness? Each creature's stock benefits from its own particular approach.

The bits we add to vegetables and water:

Chicken

You can simply use the carcass of your roast chicken, or your butcher will be able to supply you with chicken bones. Chicken wings are particularly good for stock, as are the giblets and neck if your chicken comes with them. Chicken should simmer 1½ to 2 hours.

Duck and Goose

These should come with their giblets and neck. Use these, and once you have eaten your bird you can use the carcass. Similarly with game birds: hang on to their little frames once you have eaten the flesh, and pop them in the stockpot. These, too, should simmer 1½ to 2 hours.

Veal

All good butchers will have veal bones. Ask them to cut them up slightly, allowing the goodness from the heart of the bones to emerge and enrich your stock. Roast the bones to a golden brown in the oven before putting them in the pot with the vegetables (red onions would be appropriate here) and water. Because of the size of the bones this stock will need to simmer longer than the others, about 3 hours. At this point you have veal stock that you can use as is or reduced.

I myself am not a fan of the brown sticky reductions (*jus*) that many chefs seem partial to, so the following is as brown and sticky as I get—you can get a lot stickier. Brown a new selection of vegetables (including red onion) in a little oil in a pan, then pour in red wine (how much depends on how much stock you have, so at this point you have to make an educated guess as to how much wine your pot needs—between a quarter and a third of the volume of stock) and allow this to reduce by two-thirds. Now add the veal stock. Bring this to a simmer and allow it to reduce by half (stop if it seems to be getting too viscous). Strain out the vegetables and you now have a rich brown veal reduction.

Fish

If you are not filleting fish at home ask your fishmonger for the bones and heads of non-oily fish and remove their gills. I am sure if you ask nicely your fishmonger will do this for you. This may prove difficult, as the fish store seems to be disappearing, in which case, buy yourself some cheap white but not fatty fish. If you are lucky enough to come by it, conger eel is very good. As regards the vegetables, in the case of fish stock I stick to the green and white varieties. In a little oil sweat your heads, bones, or fish bits, allowing them to color but not burn. Add the vegetables and water. Bring to a simmer, being careful not to boil them, which will give a harsh fish flavor; 45 to 60 minutes should do.

If you're planning to eat crabs, lobsters, langoustines, even prawns, keep all their shells, as they make a splendid stock. Place the shells in a pot and crush with a hammer, or the end of a heavy wooden rolling pin, until you have a shelly pulp. In this case, chop your vegetables a mite finer than I have previously recommended, and sweat them in a little oil, not browning, until they are soft and sweet. Add a couple of canned plum tomatoes (not enough to make it tomatoey), crushing them in your hands.

Add the shell pulp and sweat until you smell splendid shellfish things. Add water and simmer until the shells have released their flavor, 1½ to 2 hours. When it comes time to strain, ladle the broth and pulp into a sieve and bash it through with the bowl of the ladle, then discard the dry beaten remains in the sieve.

Chickpea

The water you have cooked chickpeas in makes an excellent vegetarian stock.

Remember: if you have boiled a chicken, ham, or beef, do not throw away the broth. You have created a stock for the next day.

Clarification

Once you have your finished stock you have the further option of clarifying it, which is the process of completely clearing it of fat and particles.

Some would say the perfect broth should have glistening spots of fat on the surface, to be sopped up with your bread. Certainly clarification is not essential, and then again, sometimes there is a certain splendor in a completely clear broth.

Here is a basic clarification recipe.

1 pound raw lean flesh from the same creature as your stock (this helps the flavor of your stock; the clarification might very slightly dent its flavor)

1 large or 2 small leeks, cleaned

2 egg whites and their shells

2 quarts stock (cold, preferably fridge cold)

In a food processor whizz the meat, leeks, and egg whites and shells into a pulp (if you have no processor, chop your meat, eggshells, and leek very finely and mix into fork-whisked egg whites). Whisk this mixture into the cold stock in a pan, place on the heat, and bring this up to a gentle simmer. Do not stir again. What will be happening is similar to making coffee in a plunger pot but in reverse. The meat and egg forms a sieve layer which will rise through the stock, collecting any

detritus on its way until it forms as a crust on top of the stock. This is why the most gentle of simmering is required, otherwise the crust will break up and be boiled back into the stock.

Once the crust has become reasonably firm, keep the pan on a gentle heat, otherwise the crust will sink, and lift off with a slotted spoon. Finally, if your stock is not clear, then complete the process by straining the stock through cheesecloth or a very fine sieve.

SOUP

PUMPKIN AND BACON SOUP

A dish suitable for a large autumnal gathering. One pumpkin will feed many. For preference, choose an organic one, with a whitish green skin that feels very hard; they're often available from health-food shops and some supermarkets.

olive oil

3 onions, peeled and chopped

3 leeks, cleaned and chopped

5 garlic cloves, peeled and chopped

2¼ to 2½ pounds smoked streaky bacon (see page 79), cubed or in chunks (keep rind in one piece)

4 canned whole tomatoes

1 pumpkin, peeled and seeded

3 bay leaves

a bundle of thyme and curly parsley tied together

at least 3¾ quarts ham or chicken stock

sea salt and freshly ground black pepper

Put a good dose of olive oil into your pot, add the chopped vegetables, and cook but do not brown. Add your chopped bacon and its rind. When these have released their fat, squish the tomatoes in your hands and add them, giving your dish a slight blush. Let all this cook down until you feel that they have really got to know each other, a gentle 25 minutes or so. While this is happening, chop your pumpkin into approximately 1-inch chunks. Add these and let them cook for 5 to 10 minutes. Then add the bay leaves and the thyme and parsley bundle. Now add the stock, enough so that you end up with an Arctic Sea of soup with icebergs of pumpkin bobbing about in your broth. Simmer until the pumpkin is soft and giving, but not falling apart (though a little disintegration is not a bad thing), say 30 to 40 minutes. Season with salt and pepper and serve hot.

PEA AND PIG'S EAR SOUP

This is based on a very dour recipe—dried peas, pig's ears, and water, the ear giving a certain body to the soup—but it is no less delicious for that.

1½ quarts flavorsome ham stock (preferably the water you boiled a ham in or a ham bone plus a head of garlic, skin on)

1 pound dried green split peas

2 pig's ears (ask your butcher, as these should not be hard to obtain; singe off as much hair as you can)

2 onions, peeled

sea salt and freshly ground black pepper

vegetable oil for frying

If you're using stock, bring it to a boil in a pan with the split peas, ears, and onions, and then simmer until the peas are soft and cooked to a thick soupy consistency (approximately 3 hours). If it starts to get too thick add more stock or water. If you have a ham bone, just cover this with water, add your garlic, split peas, ears, and onions, and cook the same way as with stock, though it will probably need some skimming. Add more water if it is getting too thick. Season with salt and pepper. Remove the onions, and if you have taken that route the head of garlic and the ham bone.

Extract the ears from the soup, rinse them, and dry them carefully. Allow them to cool and firm up, then slice very thinly. Heat the vegetable oil in a deep frying pan (or deep-fryer if you have one) and drop the ears in. Be careful, as even if dry they are likely to spit. Stir to avoid their sticking in one great mass. When crispy remove from the oil and lay on paper towels to drain off excess fat.

Serve the soup hot. On top of each bowl place a cluster of crispy ear.

If you have any boiled ham left up your sleeve you could incorporate small chunks in your soup.

CHICKEN BROTH AND WILD GARLIC

This is a very soothing, clear broth, ideal if you are feeling a little frail.

EITHER 1 chicken (the breast and meat from the legs removed and kept for the clarification) and 12 wings

OR the liquor from a boiled chicken you have eaten previously, and 2 extra chicken breasts

2 carrots, peeled and roughly chopped

2 stalks of celery, roughly chopped

2 onions, peeled and roughly chopped

2 leeks, cleaned and roughly chopped

1 head of garlic, skin on

a bundle of fresh herbs (bay leaf, curly parsley, thyme, rosemary) tied together

black peppercorns

sea salt

1 whole fresh chile (optional, but a good addition, and if kept whole it will give a subliminal warmth, a mysterious frisson)

a bundle of wild garlic leaves, roughly chopped (you can buy these in good green-grocers or pick them yourself) and tied together

If you're using the chicken carcass, place the bones and wings in a big pan and cover with water. Bring to a boil, skim off the scum, and reduce to a simmer (a rolling boil churns the scum back into the broth).

If you're using the liquor, start here.

Add your vegetables and herbs, peppercorns and salt to taste, and the chile if using. Simmer for 2½ hours, skimming as necessary. Strain, allow to cool, and then clarify using the method on page 5.

Once you have your clear broth, reheat, meanwhile placing the garlic leaves in the bottom of the soup bowl or bowls. Pour the hot soup over these, give them a few moments to get to know each other, then eat.

LEEK, POTATO, AND OYSTER SOUP

You will need a blender for this recipe, as part of the joy of the dish is the smooth velvety soup within which lurks the oyster.

7 tablespoons unsalted butter

9 good leeks, minimally trimmed to keep all the green, washed, and sliced

1 onion, peeled and sliced

5 cloves of garlic, peeled and chopped

4 potatoes, peeled and chopped

2 quarts light fish or chicken stock

sea salt and freshly ground black pepper

12 medium Pacific oysters (it is best you shuck these yourself, as you want to catch every last drop of oyster juice in a bowl)

In a pan large enough to take all the ingredients, melt the butter and sweat your leeks, onion, and garlic, avoiding any browning. When these are giving, add the potato and cook with the leek mixture for 8 minutes, again avoiding browning. Then add the stock and bring to a gentle boil. When the potato is cooked, season with salt and pepper. Now purée the soup in a blender and return it to a clean pan on the heat. Just before eating add the oyster liquor to the soup and place two oysters in each soup bowl. Pour the hot soup over the oysters and eat.

ONION SOUP AND BONE MARROW TOAST

duck fat or unsalted butter

4¼ to 4½ pounds onions, peeled, cut in half, and sliced

1 bottle (750ml) good cider (excellent cider brewed in Normandy should be available in good liquor stores)

3½ cups good veal stock (or if by chance you have some, duck stock)

2 to 2¼ pounds veal marrowbones

8 slices white bread

olive oil

sea salt and freshly ground black pepper

a handful of chopped curly parsley

In a pan large enough to take the other ingredients, melt the duck fat or butter and cook your onions. This time we want them to achieve a soft, sweet brownness (no burning). This is not a process you should rush; it will take up to 1 hour. Once achieved, add the cider and stock, bring to a simmer, and cook for 30 minutes. While this is happening, roast your marrowbones in a hot 450°F oven until the marrow is loose, not flowing out of the bones. Sprinkle the bread with olive oil and toast in the oven. Season the soup with salt and pepper.

When the bones are ready, hold them with a kitchen towel, scoop out their delicious marrow, and spread it on the crispy toast. Sprinkle with coarse sea salt. Serve the soup in deep soup bowls and top with the bone marrow toast. Finish off with a healthy topping of parsley, dropped in the dump-truck style (rather than sprinkled) onto the floating toast. Now eat.

CURLY PARSLEY As the swish, swish, swish of bunches of flat Italian parsley is to be heard in kitchens across the land, it seems time to celebrate the strength and character of the indigenous curly parsley. Its expression of chlorophyll and well being, strong flavor, slightly prickly texture, and its structural abilities enable such things as Parsley Sauce (page 66).

COCK-A-LEEKIE

We made a version of this recently at St. John, and it was so surprising and good that even though it is an old classic I thought I should include this version. I hope that no one will take offense if it seems to break with hundreds of years of cock-a-leekie culture. This is more than a soup; in fact it would happily pass as a meal in itself.

BRISKET

2 to 2¼ pounds brined beef
   brisket (brined as on
   page 76 for 10 to 12 days,
   or corned beef brisket
   from the butcher)

2 onions, peeled and chopped

2 carrots, peeled

2 leeks, cleaned and chopped

2 bay leaves

10 black peppercorns

a bundle of thyme and curly
   parsley tied together

CHICKEN

1 free-range chicken, or
   capon if available (slit the
   skin where the legs meet
   the body)

2 onions, peeled

2 leeks, cleaned

2 stalks of celery

2 bay leaves

10 black peppercorns

a bundle of thyme

a few sprigs of curly parsley

2 sprigs of rosemary

Brisket

Place the brisket and its accompanying vegetables and herbs in a pan and cover with fresh water. Bring to a boil, then straightaway reduce to a very gentle simmer, skimming constantly. This should take about 2½ hours to cook, but always check with a knife how giving the meat is. Allow the beef to cool in the broth.

Chicken

Place the chicken in a pan with its team of vegetables and herbs, bring to a boil, then place a lid on the pan and remove from the heat. Allow to cool in the stock. This will make for a moist chicken, necessary as it is to be cooked again.

Remove the beef and chicken from their stocks and cut into pieces, not too small but just so it's possible to eat them with a spoon. Strain both stocks, then add the beef stock to the chicken stock to taste. Remember, the beef stock will be quite salty, so be cautious—it may not take much. (A slight salt undertone is a good thing, though, as it plays very well with the sweet prunes we shall add at the end.)

5 leeks, cleaned and sliced
   across

the smallest dash of duck fat
   or olive oil

24 prunes with their pits
   (preferably Agen prunes
   from France, if you can
   find them)

If your combined stock is cloudy, or you are anxious about its aesthetic nature, clarify, as on page 5.

Finishing

Now, in a pan large enough to construct your soup, sweat your sliced leeks in the duck fat or olive oil for about 8 minutes, so as to bring out their sweet leeky nature, but not to lose their crunch. Pour in the stock. Add the chopped chicken and beef, bring to a gentle simmer, and let the meat heat through thoroughly. Three minutes before serving add the prunes, just giving them time to puff up. Don't pit the prunes.

Serve in big bowls with much bread at hand. Warn your guests about the pits.

NEW SEASON GARLIC AND BREAD SOUP

For the early months of spring you can get fresh garlic before it is dried. It has a longer, greener stem, giving you the flavor of garlic with a youthful nature. A food mill is very useful for this recipe—in fact a food mill is useful all the time.

8 fresh heads of garlic,
    skin on

1 quart chicken stock

sea salt and freshly ground
    black pepper

a healthy handful of chunks,
    without crust, of
    yesterday's—if not even
    the day before's—white
    bread

Place the garlic in the stock and bring to a boil, then reduce to a simmer and cook until the garlic is cooked soft—approximately 40 minutes. Then pass the garlic through the food mill (if you have no food mill, press it through a sieve). Mix the garlic pulp back into the stock and season with salt and pepper. Reheat and throw in the bread a couple of minutes before serving, so it has just long enough to sop up the soup but not fall apart.

SALADS

GRILLED JERUSALEM ARTICHOKE, RED ONION, AND OLIVES

TO SERVE FOUR

An autumnal, textural salad.

6 Jerusalem artichokes, washed but not peeled

sea salt

3 red onions, peeled and quartered

extra-virgin olive oil

a splash of balsamic vinegar

freshly ground black pepper

2 bunches of watercress, woody stalks trimmed off

a handful of small Arbequina olives, or firm green olives, e.g., Luque Royals, so they give a *gnya* to the salad

a handful of chopped curly parsley

a splash of Vinaigrette (page 161)

Boil the artichokes in salted water for 20 minutes until they are giving but not collapsing, then allow to cool. Slice lengthwise about ⅜ inch thick, and put to one side. Meanwhile toss the onions in some olive oil and balsamic vinegar, season with salt and pepper, and roast in a medium to hot 375°F oven until soft and sweet. Allow them to cool slightly. Mix the watercress, olives, and parsley (parsley acts as a great marrier of disparate parts in a salad, the dating agency of the salad world).

To grill the artichokes, either use a cast-iron grill pan or cook them over a barbecue, as it is that nutty seared flavor we are after. They should need no more than 2 to 3 minutes each side, as long as your grill pan or barbecue is hot. Keep an eye on them.

Add them to the other ingredients while warm, add the vinaigrette, toss, and serve.

HOW TO EAT RADISHES AT THEIR PEAK

bunches of breakfast radishes (the radishes that are an elongated round with a red top and a white tip) with healthy leaves, gently washed in cold water and shaken dry

coarse sea salt

good unsalted butter

Vinaigrette (page 161)

Pile your intact radishes onto a plate and have beside them a bowl of coarse sea salt and the good butter. To eat, add a knob of butter to your radish with a knife and a sprinkle of salt, then eat. Have a bowl for the discarded leaves and once you have finished the bulbs dress the leaves with as much vinaigrette as seems appropriate and toss then eat this wonderfully peppery salad.

SALT Always look for sea salt. Such things as table salt have that twang of the chemical industry about them. Experiment with sea salts as they can vary dramatically in shape and flavor. It's amazing how appropriate a particular salt can be to a certain dish.

SNAILS AND OAK LEAF LETTUCE

TO SERVE FOUR

You can pick the snails for this salad yourself. I have done this, though it is quite emotional. A few years ago on Tiree in the Hebrides we collected a positive feast's worth of snails, but what was to follow was too much for one of our party. You have to starve them, so they were left in a bucket covered with pierced plastic wrap to prevent escape and left to purge. Days seemed to pass watching the poor captive snails leaving trails of snail poo on the sides of the bucket. Eventually someone cracked and freed them, much to everyone's relief. If you are of harder heart and can get over this difficult stage, which takes about four days, you should then par-boil your snails for about 20 minutes. Remove them from their shells with a pin. (Alternatively, you can replace them in their shells and smother them with butter, garlic, and parsley.) Simmer for 1 hour, by which point they will be ready for the salad. There are American snail farms now, so fresh snails are available.

6 shallots, peeled and finely chopped

8 cloves of garlic, peeled and finely chopped

a splash of olive oil

1 cup red wine

1 large or 2 small heads of oak leaf lettuce (a soft, flappy lettuce with dark red patches and a very faint nuttiness to it), washed and separated but not shredded!

4 pieces of toast (bread sprinkled with extra-virgin olive oil and baked in the oven until crispy)

sea salt and freshly ground black pepper

24 snails, prepared

a big handful of chopped curly parsley

a splash of Vinaigrette

Fry the shallots and garlic in the oil until soft, then add the wine and reduce. While this is happening prepare the base for your salad: put the lettuce into a bowl with the toast slightly broken. When the wine has reduced so that you have a red moving gunge in your pan, season with salt and pepper and toss your snails in the mixture so they are thoroughly heated through. Add the snail mixture to the salad bowl, with the parsley and vinaigrette, toss thoroughly, and serve straightaway.

DECONSTRUCTED PICCALILLI

Traditionally, piccalilli is a spirited yellow crunchy vegetable pickle. This salad was created by my sous-chef, Dorothy Harrison. Not too surprisingly, it goes very well with cold meats or oily fish, as well as being a fine dish eaten by itself.

DRESSING

1 teaspoon sugar

a splash of red wine vinegar

2 teaspoons prepared English mustard

2 cloves of garlic, peeled and thoroughly crushed

⅞ cup extra-virgin olive oil

sea salt and freshly ground black pepper

SALAD

1 head of cauliflower, broken into generous florets

1 cucumber, cut into 3 sections, then sliced in half lengthwise, then each half cut into 3 long wedges

1 red onion, peeled, cut in half, and very thinly sliced

1¼ pounds haricots verts, topped and tailed and blanched in boiling salted water for 3 minutes

a handful of capers (extra-fine if possible)

To make the dressing, dissolve the sugar in the red wine vinegar, mix with the other ingredients, and season with salt and pepper.

To create the salad simply toss the vegetables and capers in the dressing and serve.

CUCUMBER, MUSTARD, AND DILL

This goes very well with such things as cured salmon, mackerel, and smoked cod's roe, or is very happily eaten by itself.

3 cucumbers, peeled, sliced in half lengthwise, and seeds removed (a teaspoon is the ideal cucumber gutter)

1 generous teaspoon coarse sea salt (Maldon salt is ideal)

MUSTARD DRESSING

1 teaspoon sugar

1 generous teaspoon white wine vinegar

2 generous teaspoons Dijon mustard

extra-virgin olive oil

freshly ground black pepper

a small bunch of dill, feathery leaves picked from the stems

I am normally a great believer in slicing things straight across, but the peeled and seeded cucumber is an exception; ⅜-inch slices cut at an angle will give strange wonderful shapes (hopefully).

Place the cucumbers in a colander, add the sea salt, and stir it into the cucumber pieces gently with your hands (what we are doing is drawing moisture out of the cucumbers, to achieve a crunch with a giving resistance, so one must be careful not to add too much salt because having to rinse the cucumbers later will detract from the process). Leave the salted cucumbers for 1 hour, and in the meantime make the mustard dressing.

Dissolve the sugar (this should not be a sweet dressing; its presence should be subliminal) in the vinegar in a bowl, then spoon in the mustard. Mix thoroughly. Then, gently, mixing all the while, add the olive oil, maintaining an emulsified dressing. Season with the pepper.

Now roughly chop your dill. Shake the excess salty water off the cucumbers, and tip the cucumber pieces out onto a clean kitchen towel. Pat dry. Put the cucumbers into a bowl, add the dressing and dill, mix, and serve.

SKATE, CHICORY, AND ANCHOVY

When poached and allowed to grow cold, skate sets beautifully into a firm but giving fish whose natural structure shreds perfectly for our salad-making purposes.

POACHING BROTH

1 cup white wine

zest of 1 lemon

1 head of fennel, sliced

1 onion, peeled and sliced

2 stalks of celery, chopped

1 head of garlic, chopped in
   half, skin on

black peppercorns to taste

a bunch of curly parsley tied
   together

sea salt

1 skate wing, 1½ to
   1¾ pounds (get your
   fishmonger to skin it for
   you, both sides)

ANCHOVY DRESSING

20 anchovy fillets

8 cloves of garlic, peeled

a healthy splash of red wine
   vinegar

⅔ cup extra-virgin olive oil

freshly ground black pepper

To make your poaching broth mix all the ingredients together and add enough water to cover your skate. Bring it up to a boil and then turn the heat down to a simmer. Slip your skate wing into the poaching pan and cook for approximately 10 minutes (check that the flesh comes away from the bone), then turn off the heat and allow to cool in the liquor.

2 heads of chicory (also called
curly endive; if you can get
puntarella, a vegetable
particular to Rome that
looks like thin green celery,
splendid and bitter, do), or
3 heads of Belgian endive,
rinsed and chopped

a bunch of rocket (arugula),
leaves picked from the
stem; if not available
replace with watercress or
other green peppery leaves

a handful of chopped curly
parsley

a small handful of capers
(extra-fine if possible)

When cold remove the skate from the liquor and pull
the flesh from the bone. It should come away in easy
strips. Now make your dressing: either whizz all the
ingredients in a food processor or pound them in a
mortar with a pestle.

Bring together the skate, chicory, rocket (arugula),
parsley, capers, and the dressing (caution—there may
be too much, so do not add it all at once), and toss.

MUSSELS, CUCUMBER, AND DILL

TO SERVE FOUR

a splash of olive oil

2 onions, peeled and finely chopped

2 stalks of celery, finely chopped

sea salt and freshly ground black pepper

half a bunch of fresh thyme tied together

4 pounds mussels

⅓ bottle of dry white wine

THE SALAD

1 cucumber

1 red onion, peeled, cut in half, and very thinly sliced

a bunch of dill, feathery leaves picked from the stems

a small handful of extra-fine capers

a splash of mussel liquor

a splash of extra-virgin olive oil

juice of 1 lemon

sea salt and freshly ground black pepper

In a lidded pan large enough to fit the mussels, put a splash of oil, heat it up, add the vegetables, and let them fry for a couple of minutes—watch that they do not brown. Season heartily with salt and pepper, as you still have the mussels and wine to come, and add the thyme, then your mussels and the wine. Stir so they all get to meet the mixture, place the lid on the pan, and cook the mussels, now and then giving the pan a shake. When the mussels open they are cooked. Remove from the heat and allow to cool.

Pluck the mussels from their shells, and strain and reserve the liquor.

To make the salad, cut the cucumber into 2½-inch lengths, then split in half, then cut into 3 pieces lengthwise, aiming the knife blade into the center of the cucumber. When brought together the pieces should resemble a pile of kindling, rather than cucumber matchsticks. Now mix all the salad ingredients with the reserved liquor and the mussels together and serve. The orange mussels next to the pale green cucumber flesh is very satisfactory.

ANCHOVY, LITTLE GEM, AND TOMATO

Amazingly uplifting powers for a simple salad.

6 tomatoes, the happiest you
    can find (it is possible to
    find tomatoes on the vine)

sea salt and freshly ground
    black pepper

olive oil

a handful of chopped curly
    parsley

16 good anchovy fillets in oil,
    separated but kept whole

2 heads of Little Gem lettuce,
    (tight, small crunchy
    lettuce, 3 to 4 inches high,
    2 to 3 inches across),
    washed and separated, not
    shredded

a splash of Vinaigrette
    (page 161)

Slice the tomatoes in half lengthwise, sprinkle with salt, pepper, and oil, and roast in a medium 350°F oven for approximately 20 minutes. This will soften and slightly dry them, intensifying and sweetening their flavor. Allow to cool.

Mix all the ingredients in a bowl and eat.

WARM SALT COD, LITTLE GEM, AND TOMATO

This may sound similar to the preceding Anchovy, Little Gem, and Tomato salad, but it is fundamentally different. We salt our own cod, which has not been dried, so it is firm but has not developed that peculiarly hairy nature that is ideal for other dishes. This is a dish you have to start a week in advance.

IN ADVANCE COOKING

1½ cups coarse sea salt

1 pound cod fillet, in one piece, skinned

6 tomatoes

sea salt and freshly ground black pepper

olive oil

2 heads of Little Gem lettuce, leaves separated and washed

a healthy spoonful of Aïoli (page 162)

a handful of chopped curly parsley

A week before you want your salad, find a plastic container in which your cod will fit, also remembering this has to sit in your fridge for 6 days. Line the base of the container with a layer of sea salt, lay the cod fillet on top, then cover it with more sea salt. Cover with plastic wrap or a lid and place in the fridge.

On the sixth day remove the cod from the salt and rinse under gentle running water, then soak in clean water for 12 hours, changing it regularly.

Slice the tomatoes in half lengthwise, sprinkle with salt, pepper, and oil, and roast in a medium 350°F oven for approximately 20 minutes. This will soften and slightly dry them, intensifying and sweetening their flavor. Allow to cool, and reserve the cooking juices.

Place the Little Gem leaves and tomato halves in a bowl and mix the remaining oily roast-tomato juice with the spoonful of aïoli for your dressing.

When all is ready, bring a pan of fresh water up to a gentle simmer. Chop your cod into 1-inch cubes and poach them in your simmering water for 5 minutes. If they fall apart slightly, do not worry, they will still taste delicious. Gently remove with a slotted spoon, shake off the water, and add to the other ingredients waiting in the bowl. Dress with your tomato-aïoli dressing, and add the handful of parsley. Carefully but thoroughly toss the salad and eat.

WARM PIG'S HEAD

The flesh from a pig's head is flavorsome and tender. Consider, its cheeks have had just the right amount of exercise and are covered in just the right enriching layer of fat to ensure succulent cooking results, and the snout has the lip-sticking quality of not being quite flesh nor quite fat, the perfect foil to the crunch of the crispy ear.

1 pig's head

2 bunches of wild rocket (arugula), trimmed (if not available replace with watercress or other green peppery leaves)

a bunch of sorrel, leaves picked from the stems

a big handful of curly parsley, finely chopped

a handful of cornichons, chopped

a handful of whole extra-fine capers

a handful of chunks of yesterday's white bread

DRESSING

extra-virgin olive oil

1 generous teaspoon Dijon mustard

a healthy splash of red wine vinegar

2 cloves of garlic, crushed

sea salt

freshly ground black pepper

Cook the head as for Brawn (page 39) except without the trotters. Cut the ears off so they can be rescued from the pot if there is any sign of the flesh falling off the cartilage. As soon as they're done, remove them from the pot, allow them to cool and firm up, then slice very thinly and fry as on page 43. Test the pig's head with a knife, and when the cheeks are coming away from the bone, remove it from the pot. While still hot, remove the flesh from the pig's skull, peel and slice the tongue, and shred the meat. Then dress and toss with the other ingredients and top off with the crispy ear and serve while still warm.

OX TONGUE AND BREAD

Sixteen ½-inch cubes of yesterday's white bread with crust removed

a healthy dollop of Green Sauce (page164)

16 thin slices of cold boiled corned ox tongue, like little angels' wings (one tongue will supply this and more)

8 spring onions or scallions, trimmed

2 bunches of wild rocket (arugula), trimmed (if not available replace with watercress or other green peppery leaves)

a bunch of sorrel, leaves picked from the stems

8 young borage leaves, if you can get them (borage is an herb with the taste of cucumbers, best known for its blue flowers)

a splash of Vinaigrette (page 161), or extra-virgin olive oil and lemon juice if needed

Place the bread cubes in your salad bowl with the Green Sauce, so they have a chance to absorb some of it. Then gently toss the rest of the ingredients in the bowl, trying to keep the slices of tongue reasonably intact. If it seems a wee bit dry, loosen with an extra splash of vinaigrette or oil and lemon juice.

ROCKET Rocket (arugula), a leaf that went mad with Parmesan in a salad and the global passion for Italian food, was something we considered delicate and exotic until we discovered what a hardy leaf it is and how happily it will grow in the English climate. In fact, I've brushed snow off it in my mum's garden and we still had salad for lunch.

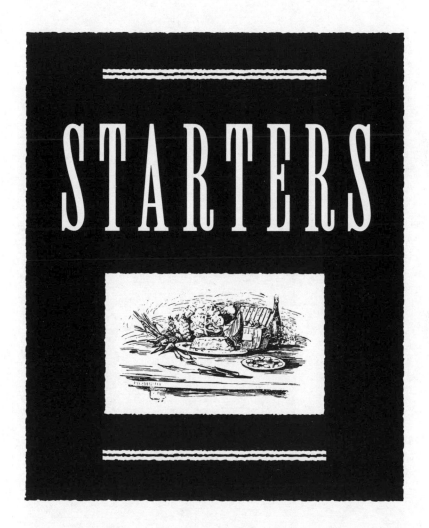

STARTERS

(Smaller But Often Sustaining Dishes)

ROAST BONE MARROW AND PARSLEY SALAD

This is the one dish that does not change on the menu at St. John. The marrowbone comes from a calf's leg; ask your butcher to keep some for you. You will need teaspoons or long thin implements to scrape your marrow out of the bone at the table.

Do you recall eating Raisin Bran for breakfast? The raisin-to-bran-flake ratio was always a huge anxiety, to a point, sometimes, that one was tempted to add extra raisins, which inevitably resulted in too many raisins, and one lost that pleasure of discovering the occasional sweet chewiness in contrast to the branny crunch. When administering such things as capers, it is very good to remember Raisin Bran.

twelve 3-inch pieces of veal marrowbone

a healthy bunch of flat-leaf parsley, leaves picked from the stems

2 shallots, peeled and very thinly sliced

1 modest handful of capers (extra-fine if possible)

DRESSING

juice of 1 lemon

extra-virgin olive oil

a pinch of sea salt and freshly ground black pepper

a good supply of toast

coarse sea salt

Put the marrowbone pieces in an ovenproof frying pan and place in a hot 450°F oven. The roasting process should take about 20 minutes, depending on the thickness of the bone. You are looking for the marrow to be loose and giving, but not melted away, which it will do if left too long (traditionally the ends would be covered to prevent any seepage, but I like the coloring and crispness at the ends).

Meanwhile lightly chop your parsley, just enough to discipline it, mix it with the shallots and capers, and at the last moment, dress the salad.

Here is a dish that should not be completely seasoned before leaving the kitchen, rendering a last-minute seasoning unnecessary by the actual eater; this, especially in the case of coarse sea salt, gives texture and uplift at the moment of eating. My approach is to scrape the marrow from the bone onto the toast and season with coarse sea salt. Then a pinch of parsley salad on top of this and eat. Of course once you have your pile of bones, salad, toast, and salt it is diner's choice.

STARTERS

CURED BEEF AND CELERIAC

This curing process can also be used on a fillet of venison.

1½ cups coarse sea salt

3 cups sugar

10 sprigs of rosemary

1 fillet of beef (ask your butcher to trim it)

a handful of finely cracked black pepper

1 head of celeriac, peeled

juice of 1 lemon

1½ tablespoon Dijon mustard

4 tablespoons crème fraîche

sea salt and freshly ground black pepper

Mix the salt and sugar together. Take a plastic container into which your fillet will fit uncured and which will fit in your fridge, and place 5 sprigs of rosemary in the bottom. Generously cover with half of the salt and sugar mix, lay the fillet on this, then cover with the rest of the mix (if you have not got enough of the salt and sugar mixture, simply make up some more, 40 percent salt to 60 percent sugar). Nestle the rest of the rosemary into this. Cover the container and leave in the fridge for 3 days. Remove the fillet from the now damp salt and sugar, rinse under cold running water, and dry with a clean cloth. When dry, take the pepper and rub the firm fillet all over; this should remove any remaining moisture and give an *oomph* to the meat. Wrap in plastic wrap and keep in the fridge until you use it (this is not a long curing process and as a result the meat will not keep for more than a week and should be refrigerated).

Slice the celeriac very thinly, using the width of a match as a rough guide (a mandoline is very useful for this), then lay a manageable pile of slices flat and slice again into matchsticks. If you don't have a mandoline, do not fear, you can easily achieve matchstick strips of celeriac with a knife. As you go, squeeze lemon juice over your growing mound of celeriac strands to prevent them going brown. Fold the Dijon mustard and crème fraîche gently together—don't beat, as the cream will lose its structure. Season with salt and pepper, and mix this through the celeriac.

To serve the beef, slice thinly across. You will have beautiful dark red flesh—the color of a fine Old Master comes to mind. The spirited white celeriac makes a splendid accompaniment.

If you don't eat it that day, it will be fine the next if kept in the fridge.

GRILLED MARINATED CALF'S HEART

This is a wonderfully simple, delicious dish, the heart not, as you might imagine, tough as old boots because of all the work it does, but in fact firm and meaty but giving.

1 calf's heart

a healthy splash of balsamic
  vinegar

coarse sea salt

freshly ground black pepper

chopped fresh thyme, leaves
  only

Trim the heart of anything that looks like sinew (this is easy enough to spot) and excess fat (which tends to be around the open top of the heart), and remove any blood clots lurking in the ventricles. Slice the heart open so you can lay it flat and complete the cleaning process. Then cut it into pieces 1 inch square, up to ¼ inch thick; if the flesh suddenly gets thick, simply slice it in half horizontally through the meat.

Toss the pieces of heart in the balsamic vinegar, salt, pepper, and thyme. Leave to marinate for 24 hours.

Now for cooking you need a cast-iron grill pan or a barbecue. Get it very hot and apply the heart: it will take about 3 minutes each side. Serve with a spirited salad of your choice, e.g. watercress, shallot and bean, or raw leek.

PIG'S TROTTERS These are one of the most gastronomically useful extremities. If your butcher has pork, there must be a trotter lurking somewhere. They bring to a dish an unctuous, lip-sticking quality unlike anything else. The joy of finding a giving nodule of trotter in a dish!

BRAWN (HEADCHEESE)

A splendid dish, a slowly cooked pig's head, the flesh pulled from the skull and set in its own jelly; sliced thinly, a fine lunch. You can use the pig's ears to make the Sorrel, Chicory, and Crispy Ear Salad (page 43), which is an ideal accompaniment.

1 pig's head, rinsed thoroughly

4 pig's trotters (see box, page 38)

2 onions, peeled

2 carrots, peeled

2 leeks, cleaned

2 stalks of celery

2 heads of garlic, skin on

zest of 2 lemons

a healthy splash of red wine vinegar

a bundle of fresh herbs tied together

2 bay leaves

a scant handful of black peppercorns (tied in cheese-cloth—or you will be picking them out of the cooked meat forever)

sea salt

Place the head and trotters in a large pot, cover with water, and add all the other ingredients except salt. As soon as you have brought it up to a boil, reduce to a very gentle simmer, skimming as you go.

If using, extract the ears after about 1 hour, rinse them, and dry them carefully. When you can feel the cheek starting to come away from the bone (this should take about 2½ hours), remove everything from the liquor and discard the vegetables. Return the liquor to the heat to reduce by about half, then season with salt, remembering this is served cold, which subdues flavors. While still warm, pick through the trotters and pig's head, retrieving the flesh, especially peeling the tongue. The snout is neither fat nor meat; do not be discouraged, it is delicious in your brawn.

Line your terrine with plastic wrap and fill with the retrieved meats. Pour in enough of the reduced liquor just to cover, slamming the mold on the kitchen counter to shake out any air bubbles. Leave to set overnight in the fridge, and before you serve it, remove it in good time to acclimatize without being so warm it is soft and sweaty.

JELLIED TRIPE

I know there is a general mistrust of tripe; interestingly enough, this dish has produced most tripe converts. It does have a seductive nature of looking like summer on a plate, but it's not just its good looks that recommend it—it is delicious.

4 pig's trotters (see page 38)

2 heads of garlic, skin on, plus 6 cloves, peeled and finely chopped

bay leaves

a bundle of fresh thyme tied together

2 quarts good dry cider

1 cup Calvados, optional

4¼ to 4½ pounds tripe

1 scoop of duck fat

8 shallots, peeled and thinly sliced

4 carrots, peeled and thinly sliced

2 leeks, cleaned, trimmed, and thinly sliced

4 canned whole plum tomatoes

sea salt and freshly ground black pepper

Place the trotters, whole heads of garlic, bay leaves, thyme, cider, and Calvados (if using) in a pot, bring up to a boil, and reduce to a simmer. After 2 hours add the tripe. Cook for another 1 to 1½ hours, until the tripe and trotters are cooked: when you pinch them, your fingers easily go through the flesh. Remove the tripe and trotters, herbs, and garlic from the liquor, which you should leave cooking to reduce by half. Pull the flesh off the trotters while still warm and add to the tripe, discarding the bones.

Meanwhile sweat the shallots, carrots, leeks, and chopped garlic in the duck fat until softened, but not a pulp. Add the tomatoes, crushing them in your hand as you do so, and let this mixture cook for a further 20 minutes, sweetening the tomatoes (you are not looking to make a tomato dish, just bring the faintest blush). Now add the tripe and trotter flesh to the pot with a few ladles of the liquor, and season with salt and pepper—remember that this will be served cold, so slightly overcompensate. Let this cook gently together for another 30 minutes.

Line a terrine or loaf pan with plastic wrap. Spoon in the tripe, trotter, and vegetables with a slotted spoon, topping up at the end with liquid so they're just covered. Make sure, by banging the mold on the counter, you are not left with any gaps or air holes. Cover with plastic wrap and leave in the fridge overnight to set.

When firm, remove it from the fridge to acclimatize without getting too warm, and slice it as you would a terrine: you should have a beautiful cross section through a tripy weave. Serve with chicory salad dressed with Dijon mustard, red wine vinegar, extra-virgin olive oil, and capers.

ROLLED PIG'S SPLEEN

People venting their spleens has been bad press gastronomically for the organ. Please do not be deterred; spleens are a joy to cook with and eat, and the texture is not dissimilar to liver. Beautifully symmetrical, not wobbly and unmanageable, they are the perfect organ to give offal a good name. In fact they are often used in terrines, their presence overlooked in favor of more glamorous ingredients. This recipe goes a small way to redress the balance. Eat with very thinly sliced raw red onion and cornichons.

1 pig's spleen (given prior warning your butcher should have no problem obtaining it)

sea salt and freshly ground black pepper

4 sage leaves

2 slices of smoked streaky bacon (see page 79), not too thin, rind removed

chicken stock (enough to cover the spleen)

Lay your spleen out flat (it is a very neat and easy-to-use organ), and season with salt and pepper. Place your sage leaves along it, then the bacon lengthwise, roll it up, and skewer it. Place in an ovenproof dish, cover with the chicken stock, put in a medium 350°F oven for 1½ hours, then let cool in the stock. When cold it is ready to eat; you can keep it in the stock until you need it.

To serve, remove the skewer and slice into three or four slices so you get a cross section of spleen and bacon spiral.

SORREL, CHICORY, AND CRISPY EAR SALAD

SERVES EIGHT

This is a fine accompaniment for Brawn. You will need pig's ears, cooked as in the recipe on page 39.

2 pig's ears, cooked

vegetable oil for frying

2 handfuls of sorrel leaves, picked from the stems, washed and drained

two heads of chicory (see page 25)

a handful of curly parsley leaves, picked from the stems

1 generous teaspoon capers (extra-fine if possible)

Vinaigrette (page 161)

Allow the ears to cool and firm up, then slice very thinly. Heat the vegetable oil in a deep frying pan (or deep-fryer if you have one) and drop the ears in. Be careful, as even if dry they are likely to spit. Stir to avoid their sticking in one great mass. When crispy remove from the oil and lay on paper towels to drain off excess fat. Pick off the sorrel leaves, chop the chicory, and finely chop the curly parsley, add the capers, dress with a vinaigrette, and then top with the crispy ears.

CELERY SALT AND BOILED EGGS

1½ cups coarse sea salt

1 pound celeriac, peeled and grated

free-range eggs (as many as you want)

Mix the salt and celeriac, put into a plastic container, and cover. Leave in the fridge for 2 days, allowing time for the celeriac and salt to get to know each other. Then lay out the mixture in a baking pan and bake in a gentle oven at about 200°F for 2 to 3 hours until thoroughly dried out and crisp; check frequently to avoid any singeing, as this will give the celery salt a burnt taste. Grind the dried salt and celeriac in a food processor or crush in a mortar and pestle. The celery salt will keep for ages in an airtight container.

Cook your eggs in gently boiling water for 8 minutes, then cool under cold running water, which should result in a slightly yielding yolk.

Serve together. Peel your egg, dip it in the salt, and eat.

PICKLED HERRING

Two pickled herring fillets will do handsomely as a starter and three will happily pass as a light lunch. Eat with their pickled vegetables, a blob of crème fraîche, and capers. Or, allowing two fillets per person, chop the pickled herring fillets across into ½-inch sections, mix with hot sliced boiled potatoes, the pickled vegetables, and capers, dress with extra-virgin olive oil, toss, and serve while the potatoes are still warm.

8 herring

¾ cup coarse sea salt

3 cups sugar

2 cups white wine vinegar

1¼ cups water

14 whole allspice

14 black peppercorns

2 carrots, peeled and thinly sliced

3 red onions, peeled and thinly sliced

1½-inch piece of fresh horseradish, peeled and thinly sliced

3 bay leaves

To fillet the herring, lay them flat on one side, and with a thin, sharp knife cut just behind the gills until you feel the blade touch the backbone, then turn the blade toward the tail; hold the head and slip the knife tailward along the backbone. Turn the fish over and repeat the process. You may have to trim off some of the remaining herring ribs. (Or ask your fishmonger.)

Mix the salt and 1½ cups of the sugar together, and place your herring fillets in a plastic container, sprinkling this mixture between each layer. Leave in the fridge for 24 hours. This will lead to a firmer, more flavorsome final result. Next day rinse off the sugar and salt and drain the herring.

In a stainless-steel pan, heat up the vinegar, water, and the remaining sugar until the sugar is thoroughly dissolved. Remove from the heat and allow to cool. In the container in which you intend to store your pickled herring (plastic, glass, or china), layer the fillets with your spices, sliced vegetables, and bay leaves equally spread about, then cover with the cooled sugar solution. Leave for a week before eating; it will keep very well in the fridge.

DRIED SALTED PIG'S LIVER, RADISHES, AND BOILED EGGS

The salty nature of the dried salted pig's liver, the sweetness of the reduced vinegar, the soothing, steadying nature of the boiled eggs, and the pepperiness of the radishes (and hopefully their leaves) make for an extraordinary salad and a thing of beauty to boot. This recipe requires 5 weeks' advance thought.

PIG'S LIVER

1¾ cups coarse sea salt

2½ cups sugar

1 pig's liver

a handful of ground black pepper

Liver

Find a plastic, glass, or china container that will fit in your fridge and is large enough for the liver. Mix the salt and sugar and lay a healthy layer in your container. Rub the mix into the liver's nooks and crannies, then lay it on your prepared bed. Cover the liver with the remaining mix, cover it with a lid or plastic wrap, and leave in the fridge for 2 weeks (if the mixture all melts away with the juices from the liver, you may have to replenish with more dry mixture).

When the time is up, remove the liver from the mixture: it should be firm but not rock hard. Rinse it thoroughly with cold water. Dry it with a clean cloth, rub it down with black pepper, then roll and wrap it in another clean kitchen towel, tying firmly with string. Leave to hang in a cool dry airy place for at least 3 weeks.

a bunch of whole radishes
(preferably breakfast
radishes), washed, with
their leaves (if the leaves
are not happy, then rocket
[arugula], preferably wild,
will substitute)

four 8-minute boiled free-
range eggs, peeled and
chopped in halves or
quarters

8 whole spring onions or
scallions, trimmed (roll in
a hot pan with some oil
so they begin to soften,
as they act as a structural
weave through the salad)

a handful of capers (extra-
fine if possible)

a handful of chopped curly
parsley

a splash of Vinaigrette
(page 161)

a smidgen of extra-virgin
olive oil

a splash of balsamic vinegar

Salad

Slice off 16 thin round slices of dried liver. Toss all the
salad ingredients together in a bowl with the
vinaigrette. Get a frying pan hot and apply a drop of
oil. Place the liver slices in—your aim is to simply show
them the pan—then turn them over, add a healthy
splash of balsamic vinegar, and allow them to sizzle for
a moment. Remove from the heat; the liver slices
should be shimmering and slightly softened. Lay them
on top of the salad, drizzle the
remaining juices from the pan on
top, and serve immediately.

CURED HAM

This recipe has its origins in the Italian method for making *coppa*, but has been handed down in a verbal fashion from an Italian prisoner of war who took up residence in France to my previous sous-chef, Paul Hughes, then to me, and now to these pages. Inevitably, there is an element of playing telephone, with the recipe changing accordingly, so what we have here may not relate at all to how Italians make *coppa*, but it makes a fine cured ham. A collar of pork is the cut above the shoulder; you can also use the shoulder (sometimes called Boston butt), a cut with a lot of fat.

STAGE ONE

2 bottles of red wine

1 tablespoon saltpeter (if available: be careful—it is very strong and itches terribly if it comes in contact with the skin) or 1½ cups coarse sea salt

12 whole cloves

2 heads of garlic, skin on, cut in half to expose the flesh of the bulbs

12 black peppercorns

1 collar of pork, boned

STAGE TWO

4½ cups coarse sea salt mixed with 4 cups sugar

Mix all the ingredients for stage one together in a container made of glass, plastic, or china, and immerse your pork collar in the mixture. It is vital the meat is covered. Cover the container and place in the fridge for 12 days.

Now remove the collar from its winey bath, and dry thoroughly with a clean kitchen towel. Wash out your container thoroughly and dry it. Now lay some wooden strips along the bottom of the container that will lift your pork off the bottom (chopsticks are very good for this).

Rub the salt and sugar mixture for stage two into the pork, then lay it in the container on your waiting slats. Pack the rest around and on top of the collar and return it to the fridge for 2 weeks. If the salt and sugar become wet and run off the pork, make up another mix and reapply.

Stage three requires good strong arms, strong kitchen string, and cheesecloth. Remove the collar from the container, rinse with cold water, and dry thoroughly. Now forcefully roll your collar and tie tightly; this is vital for the prevention of internal mold. Wrap in the cloth and hang somewhere cool, airy, and dry for 2 months, by which point it should be ready to slice.

I am afraid this recipe is not fail-safe; nature being nature, mold and rot can strike, but please do not let this deter you, as when it works it is delicious and well worth the effort and patience. Of course, should nature turn against you, toss the ham and start over.

DUCK NECK TERRINE

TO SERVE SIX TO EIGHT

I hope you have more luck in the United States in procuring duck necks with the skin on. Duck necks are available at Chinese butchers. It can be problematic over here, but well worth the chase, as you will find.

8 duck necks, skins removed and reserved

12 duck gizzards, cleaned and trimmed, but not chopped

3 duck legs

12 ounces pork belly (see page 74), diced

coarse sea salt

half a bunch of fresh thyme

duck fat (enough to cover) at room temperature

¼ pound smoked streaky bacon (see page 79) finely cubed

ground allspice

ground mace

cracked pepper

14 ounces fatback, very thinly sliced

½ pound pitted prunes, soaked for at least 24 hours in hot tea with a healthy splash of brandy in it

Place the skinned duck necks, gizzards, and legs with the pork belly in a plastic or china container, sprinkle with salt and thyme twigs, toss around so the salt gets all around, cover, and leave in the fridge for 24 hours. Shake off the salt and thyme, lay in a baking pan and cover with duck fat. Cover with aluminum foil and place in a medium 325°F to 350°F oven until the flesh is giving and just coming away from the bone (2 to 2½ hours).

Tip into a container to cool. You should keep confit for months to develop, but in this case you are allowed to speed things along. Remove the legs and necks from the fat and pull the meat away from the bones. In a bowl mix this with the pork belly, gizzards, bacon, and enough duck fat to keep it a moving mixture, and season with allspice, mace, and pepper (salt is unnecessary because of the bacon). Remember this will be served cold, so compensate with generous seasoning.

Meanwhile, roll out a piece of plastic wrap on which you lay a regimented row of thinly sliced fatback as long as your terrine or loaf pan. Then lay a lengthwise row of your soaked prunes two-thirds of the way up the row. Then, using the plastic wrap to lift the fat, fold the top third back over the prunes, press down, and peel back the plastic wrap. Then, again using the plastic wrap, bring the other two-thirds of fat over the almost covered prunes, then gently roll the whole thing back toward you, at which point you should have a perfect prune-fat roll. Remove the plastic wrap.

Line your terrine with the duck neck skin as you would with bacon, leaving flaps hanging over the sides to cover the top. Fill the lined mold a third of the way up with the duck and pork mixture, then lay your prune roll down the middle. Cover with more mixture up to just below the top of the mold, flip over the duck's neck flaps, and top off with foil.

Line the bottom of a roasting pan with a kitchen towel folded in half (this diffuses the direct heat from the base of the pan), sit your terrine on the towel, and surround with water. Follow the height of the pan and terrine: don't go over either edge, and allow enough leeway for waves as you move the pan. Put into a medium 350°F oven for 2 hours.

Remove the pan from the oven and the terrine from the pan. Replace the foil with new foil, cut a piece of cardboard to match the opening of your terrine, place this on top, and apply weights to press the terrine. Allow to cool and put it in the fridge for 24 hours to allow it to find itself.

To serve, take it from the fridge to acclimatize, then remove it from the mould and slice: you should have something resembling a terrazzo floor with a prune eye in the middle. Serve with bread, cornichons, and red wine.

DUCK HEARTS ON TOAST

The perfect snack for the cook who has just prepared five ducks. The hearts have an amazing ducky quality.

1 slice of toast

a knob of unsalted butter

5 duck hearts (in an ideal world, otherwise as many as you can muster up)

a splash of balsamic vinegar

a splash of chicken stock

sea salt

freshly ground black pepper

Have your toast ready.

Get a frying pan very hot, pop in your knob of butter, followed by the hearts, and fry them for 4 minutes, rolling them around occasionally. Apply a splash of balsamic vinegar and chicken stock, season with salt and pepper, and let the hearts get to know the liquor for a couple of minutes. Place the hearts on the toast, leave the sauce on the heat to reduce for a moment, and pour over the toast and duck hearts. Eat.

LAMB'S BRAINS

AND

SWEETBREADS

Here are four recipes for the preparation of lamb's brains. Though I am aware they currently fall into the category of banned offal in England, I believe it is important to have the recipes written down so that when lamb's brain is freed from its sentence we shall be ready to celebrate its liberty.

Why lamb's brains? You can substitute calf's brains, but lamb's brains are the preferred cut. Although they are legal in the United States, they are very difficult to obtain. Lamb's brains are cheaper than calf's, but still delicious, creamy, and rich, and no other ingredient offers you better possibilities of the gentle give and crunch combination.

COLD LAMB'S BRAINS ON TOAST

This is a dish for those who particularly enjoy the texture of brain.

2 onions, peeled

2 carrots, peeled

2 leeks, trimmed and cleaned

2 stalks of celery

1 head of garlic, skin on

black peppercorns in cheesecloth

bay leaf

a bundle of fresh herbs tied together

4 lamb's brains, rinsed in cold water

4 pieces of bread, long rather than square

a splash of extra-virgin olive oil

Green Sauce (page 164)

sea salt

Bring a pot of water with all the stock vegetables and herbs up to a simmer and cook for 15 minutes. Then *gently* lower your lamb's brains into the pot, let them cook gently for 8 minutes, remove with a slotted spoon, and leave to cool on a clean kitchen towel. Meanwhile, toast the bread.

When the brains are cold and firm, separate the lobes, slice lengthwise about ¼ inch thick, lay in fish-scale fashion on the toast, and top with some olive oil, Green Sauce, and sea salt. The give of the brains, then the crunch of the toast, and the bite of the sauce are fantastic.

LAMB'S BRAINS AND SWEETBREADS

LAMB'S BRAIN TERRINE

This recipe is closely inspired by a recipe of Paula Wolfert who, in turn, points out she has been inspired by Lucien Vanel; so thank you, Lucien Vanel, and indeed Paula Wolfert.

As well as being delicious and textural to eat, this terrine, when sliced, beautifully exposes a cross section of a brain, caught in a meaty square. Although this may not sound it to all, it is a thing of beauty.

8 lamb's brains, rinsed thoroughly in cold water

2 cloves of garlic, peeled and chopped

2 shallots, peeled and chopped

2 duck livers

10 ounces lean pork, chopped

10 ounces lean veal, chopped

10 ounces pork fatback, chopped into chunks

1 healthy pinch of black pepper

1 healthy pinch of ground allspice

1 small pinch of ground cinnamon

1 small pinch of ground clove

1 small pinch of ground nutmeg

a splash of brandy

In gently boiling water blanch your brains for 4 minutes, then carefully remove them with a slotted spoon. Refresh them in ice-cold water, and drain on a clean kitchen towel.

In a food processor (or by hand, very finely chopping the ingredients) whizz the garlic first until it is a purée, then add the shallots and the duck livers so that they merge with the garlic purée, followed by the pork, veal, and fatback. Caution, you do not want this mixture too fine! Keep your finger near the off button. Texture is a grand thing in a terrine. Tip this into a bowl and season with spices and the splash of brandy. Mix. (Allspice, cinnamon, clove, and nutmeg are known as *quatre épices,* vital in most terrine and sausage making, as ground meat often loses its flavor and needs these spices' help to find it again.)

1¼ pounds unsmoked streaky bacon (see page 79) thinly sliced (enough to line your terrine or loaf pan and cover the top)

sea salt (but be cautious, because your bacon and your fatback may have been salted—if this is so do not add salt)

Line your terrine or loaf pan with the streaky bacon, leaving flaps to cover the top of the terrine. Place a layer of the terrine mix up to a third of the terrine's height, then run the brains down the middle all the way along, nestling them close together so everyone will have a good, brainy slice. Cover with the rest of the mix, then bring your bacon flaps over to cover the top of the terrine and cover with aluminum foil.

Fold a kitchen towel in half and lay it in a deep roasting pan (this will calm the direct heat on the bottom of the terrine), place the terrine on top of this, and surround with water up to two-thirds of the way up the mold's side, and place in a medium to hot 375°F oven for 2 hours. Use a skewer to check that the center of the terrine is hot, and if it is, remove from the oven and its watery pan. Allow to rest for a few minutes, then remove the foil and replace it with new foil. Put the terrine under pressure with some weights (see page 51) and, in this condition, once cooled let it sit in the fridge for 2 days, then eat.

DEEP-FRIED LAMB'S BRAINS

2 onions, peeled

2 carrots, peeled

2 leeks, trimmed and cleaned

2 stalks of celery

1 head of garlic, skin on

black peppercorns in
 cheesecloth

bay leaf

a bundle of fresh herbs tied
 together

6 lamb's brains, rinsed in cold
 water

all-purpose flour seasoned
 with sea salt and freshly
 ground black pepper

4 free-range eggs

1 cup milk

fine dried white breadcrumbs

vegetable oil for frying

Green Sauce (page 164)

Bring a pot of water with all the stock vegetables and herbs up to a simmer and cook for 15 minutes. Then *gently* lower your lamb's brains into the pot, let them cook gently for 6 minutes, remove with a slotted spoon, and leave to cool on a kitchen towel. When the brains are cold and firm, separate the lobes.

Meanwhile, prepare three bowls: the first with the seasoned flour; the second with the eggs and milk whisked together; the third with the breadcrumbs.

Heat up your oil for deep-frying: once you have coated the brains, you don't want to leave the crusts to get soggy.

It is a great help to have an extra pair of hands at this point for the tossing and rolling, but if they're not available, try to keep one hand dry and one eggy, otherwise you start to form great lumps of flour, egg, and bread on your hands, which will transfer to the brains.

Roll a brain in flour, then coat it in the egg mix, and finish with a roll in the breadcrumbs. With a small shake carefully set it aside for frying.

When the oil is hot pop the brains in until crisp: this will take a matter of minutes. Drain on paper towels, and serve hot with Green Sauce. The result is like biting through crunch into a rich cloud.

LAMB'S BRAINS, ENDIVE, AND SHALLOTS

4 endive (see page 25)

5 knobs of unsalted butter

juice of 1 lemon

sea salt and freshly ground black pepper

12 shallots, peeled but kept whole

olive oil

6 lamb's brains, rinsed and blanched as for frying (see page 58), lobes separated

a splash of chicken stock

a splash of sherry vinegar

a handful of capers (extra-fine if possible)

a handful of chopped curly parsley

Place the endive in an ovenproof dish just big enough to fit them, apply 4 knobs of the butter, pour over the lemon juice, and season with salt and pepper. Cover with aluminum foil and put into a medium to hot 375°F oven for 40 minutes. Remove from the oven and allow to cool. Leave the oven on.

Place the shallots in an ovenproof frying pan, toss with oil, and season. Put into the oven at the same temperature and roast until soft, sweet, and giving (approximately 20 minutes). Now get a large frying pan hot, then reduce the heat, add the remaining knob of butter, and when melted and sizzling, add the brains. Brown gently on both sides. It is important not to be too ferocious doing this, to get a reasonably even golden crispiness on your brains. Remove the brains and keep warm. Slice the endive in half lengthwise and place in the frying pan. Gently color and heat through on both sides. Add the shallots, brains, and chicken stock, and season. Raise the heat slightly and let all the ingredients get to know each other. Just before serving, add the sherry vinegar, and let this sizzle for a moment, then place on a hot plate. To serve, scatter with a subliminal showing of capers, and then parsley. Eat while hot, making sure you have some crusty white bread at hand for sopping up the juices.

SWEETBREADS

Once you have mastered this you are on your way, your sweetbreads ready to welcome any number of companions on the plate with them.

We tend to use lamb sweetbreads, mainly because of cost and the small nodule factor. This is not to put down the larger and equally delicious veal sweetbread.

1 pound lamb sweetbreads

salt and freshly ground black pepper

a pot of water (enough to happily cover the sweetbreads)

a healthy splash of white wine

cloves of garlic

a bundle of thyme and parsley tied together

black peppercorns

a splash of olive oil

a knob of unsalted butter

Rinse your sweetbreads thoroughly in cold, gently running water to remove any blood, giving them the occasional gentle shuggle to aid the cleansing process.

Bring your pot of water with its wine, herbs, and spices to a boil. Reduce to a gentle simmer. Slip your sweetbreads into the pot. Poach for 2½ minutes so they firm up slightly. Think of the finger that pushes the Pillsbury Doughboy's tummy. Your finger should push the same way.

Remove the sweetbreads from the pot, lay a kitchen towel out on a tray, and scatter the sweetbreads across it to cool and dry off.

Once the sweetbreads are cool enough to handle, peel the membrane off the little glands, a slightly fiddly process but well worth the trouble when it comes to the eating.

Now to the vital part. Get your frying pan hot, but not furiously hot. Add a splash of oil and a knob of butter. As this melts, season the sweetbreads with salt and pepper and then add to the pan. What we are looking for is a steady sizzle, not a frantic singeing, so that the sweetbreads brown to a nutty crispness all over, maintaining a giving interior. At this point they are ready to serve with a chunk of lemon—the nutty nodule, not the burnt offering or the anemic gland.

Once you have achieved the nutty nodule, there are many additions to the pan you can make, for example, a splash of chicken stock, a splash of red wine vinegar, peas, pea shoots, young fava beans, bacon, quarters of Little Gem lettuce, braised endive, mint, capers, young spinach, or watercress.

MEAT

HAM IN HAY

THIS WILL FEED TWELVE—THOUGH IF YOU ARE FEWER, WHAT BETTER THAN TO HAVE SOME LEFT OVER COLD?

The cooking of ham in hay imbues it with the most wonderful and unusual flavor, while insulating the meat from any fierce heat so that it cooks in the ideal gentle fashion, resulting in the most giving of flesh. It also fills your home with rustic, pastoral smells. To obtain your hay ask a friendly farmer if one is at hand, or just ask around—this can have surprisingly productive results. If all else fails a reliable pet shop is a good source.

You will need a pot large enough to fit a leg of pork!

a big bundle of hay (organic, for obvious reasons)

10 juniper berries

14 black peppercorns

10 cloves

6 bay leaves

1 whole fresh leg of pork with bone in; brined (page 76) for 12 to 14 days but not smoked

In a big pot make a base of hay, sprinkle on your spices and bay leaves, and lay the ham in your hay nest. Cover with more hay around and on top. Cover with water. Bring to a boil, then straightaway turn down to the gentlest simmer. Put a lid on and cook either in the oven or on top, making sure that it is not boiling too fast. Cook until tender all the way through (check by probing with a thin, sharp knife) for 3½ to 4½ hours. The hay is sadly not edible.

Serve with mashed rutabaga (if possible made with goose or duck fat). The pink ham and the orange rutabaga look like a sunset on a plate.

BOILED HAM AND PARSLEY SAUCE

Incredibly simple, but delicious and particularly beautiful on the plate. I believe it is important to have the parsley sauce in a jug on the table so the eaters can express themselves with their pouring. When buying your ham, avoid pink things in hairnets; look for organic and free range if possible. It is always good to cook a bit more than you will eat so you can have cold ham.

4½-pound piece of picnic ham, boned, rolled, and tied; brined (page 76) for 12 to 14 days but not smoked

2 stalks of celery

2 onions, peeled and stuck with 8 cloves

2 leeks, cleaned

3 bay leaves

10 black peppercorns

10 good-sized carrots, peeled but left whole (this way they stay sweeter)

PARSLEY SAUCE

7 tablespoons butter

¾ cup all-purpose flour

2½ cups milk

sea salt and freshly ground black pepper

a big bunch of curly parsley, finely chopped

Place your ham in a pot, keeping in mind you will need room for your carrots. Cover with water, add the celery, onions, leeks, bay leaves, and peppercorns. Bring gently to a boil, skim, reduce to a simmer, and cook for 2½ hours. Add your carrots.

Now make your sauce. Melt the butter in a pan, add the flour, and stir on a gentle heat—do not let it color. It's ready for the milk when it smells biscuity. Add the milk, whisking ferociously, making sure the heat's not too fierce. When you have a firm white creamy mixture, add a ladle of ham stock, and whisk again. Do this until you have reached your desired consistency. Test for seasoning. Just before serving add the chopped parsley and stir.

When the carrots are cooked you are ready to serve (if the ham is cooked and the carrots not, remove the ham from the water and turn up the heat). Slice the ham and serve on a plate with carrots and a drizzle of ham stock from the pot. Mustard is vital on the table.

You will be left with delicious ham stock for another day, and cold ham for your sandwiches.

FAVA BEANS, HAM, AND PARSLEY SAUCE

The fava bean has a difficult time. The growers here are still swayed by the village fête mentality: "the first prize goes to the largest fava bean" (by which time it's tough, dull, and starchy). Or restaurants peel off the gray-green skins, leaving a little bright green kernel, with nothing fava bean about it. Leave the fava bean alone; just pick it at the right time.

This is the most delicious way of using up the remaining boiled ham, in fact so good it is worth boiling a ham especially for the dish.

yesterday's boiled ham, cut into chunks

broth from the ham (page 66)

fava beans (as many as you want)

Parsley Sauce (page 66)

Gently warm the chunks of ham in the broth it was boiled in yesterday. Boil the beans in the ham broth. When cooked (approximately 3 minutes), drain and place the beans in a dish, nestle the warm ham into the beans, pour hot parsley sauce on the ham and beans, and eat straightaway. A joy!

BACON KNUCKLE AND PICKLED CABBAGE

SERVES FOUR AND SHOULD LEAVE YOU WITH CABBAGE LEFT OVER FOR FUTURE USE

The bacon knuckle comes from the knee joint of a pig and is brined. If you omit the knuckles and up the bacon quota, the resulting cabbage makes a very good accompaniment to pheasant or pigeon.

2 heads of cabbage

6 tablespoons coarse sea salt

20 juniper berries

4 smallish firm onions, peeled and thinly sliced

a good spoonful of duck fat

10 black peppercorns

3 bay leaves

1¼- to 1½-pound piece of smoked pork belly or smoked streaky bacon (see page 79), rind removed and sliced into four pieces

4 smoked bacon knuckles or smoked ham hocks

1 bottle of dry white wine

Thinly slice and core the cabbage with a good big knife. Find a china, glass, or plastic container that will not react with the salt (aluminum is not appropriate). Put in a layer of chopped cabbage, salt, and juniper berries, then cabbage again. Continue to fill the container in this fashion, then cover with a weighted lid to keep the cabbage submerged in its liquid. Leave somewhere warmish for 2 weeks. It will produce lots of water and when you smell it, it will smell quite *umpfy*. This is all good.

After 2 weeks, release your cabbage from its weights, drain, and rinse thoroughly. Get a thick pot, in which you next cook down your onions in the duck fat. When they are happy and soft, not brown, take off the heat. Put in a healthy layer of pickled cabbage, sprinkle on the peppercorns and bay leaves, then nestle the pork belly or bacon and the knuckles into the cabbage. Cover with more cabbage, pour your bottle of wine over this, lay on it the bacon rind, fat down, and cover tightly with aluminum foil and a lid. Pop into a gentle 300°F oven and cook for 2 to 3 hours until the knuckles are soft and giving.

Serve with boiled potatoes.

BLOOD CAKE AND FRIED EGGS

You will need to ask your butcher for the blood. Chinese butchers are a good source. It may be difficult to obtain, but it can be got. You will also need an 8-inch loaf pan lined with plastic wrap.

1 large onion, peeled and finely chopped

6 cloves of garlic, finely chopped

a dollop of duck fat

half a bunch of marjoram, leaves only, finely chopped

½ teaspoon ground mace

½ teaspoon ground allspice

1 quart fresh pig's blood

¾ cup coarse yellow cornmeal

sea salt and freshly ground black pepper

½ pound fatback (salted *lardo* will suffice), cut into ¼-inch cubes

another 2 dollops of duck fat

16 free-range eggs

In a pan large enough to take all the ingredients, sweat the onion and garlic in the duck fat until clear, soft, and giving, but not brown. Add the marjoram, spices, blood, and cornmeal and stir on a gentle heat until the blood starts to thicken to a runny porridge consistency (do not let it cook and set). It has to have a certain density or the fatback will sink to the bottom when added. At this point (not for the more squeamish cook) taste and adjust the seasoning with salt and pepper if necessary, and when happy remove the pan from the heat and add the chopped fatback. Stir to spread the fatty chunks through the blood and decant the mixture into the plastic wrap–lined loaf pan. Cover with aluminum foil and place on a flat folded kitchen towel in a deep roasting pan or dish. Surround with water (not going over the edge of the loaf pan) and bake in a gentle to medium 350°F oven for 1½ hours. Check that a skewer or sharp knife comes out clean, then remove the pan and allow the cake to cool and set (wrapped in plastic wrap it keeps very well in the fridge).

Once firm, slice into ½-inch-thick slices, get two frying pans hot, add some duck fat to them, and gently fry your slices of blood cake until heated through. In the other pan, fry a pair of eggs per person. To serve, give each plate 2 slices of fried blood cake, topped with a couple of fried eggs, and eat straightaway. It has surprising soothing qualities, this dish.

PIG'S TROTTER STUFFED WITH POTATO

TO SERVE FOUR

A good addition to this dish is very finely chopped, blanched green cabbage mixed into your mashed potatoes as well as shallots, so you are stuffing your trotter with a bubble and squeak.

4 long pig's trotters
(see page 38)

stock vegetables and herbs
(what you have on hand;
see page 3)

1 head of garlic, separated
into cloves, skin on

½ bottle of red wine

3 pounds good mashing
potatoes

sea salt

2 shallots, peeled and sliced

duck fat or olive oil

freshly ground black pepper

caul fat (your butcher should
have no problem obtaining
this for you)

Singe all the hair off the trotters, then bone them out. Chefs have likened this to being as easy as removing a kid glove, but if you don't find this, don't get disheartened. Start at the other end from the hoof, cut under the skin as close to the bone as possible (avoid cutting through the skin), work your knife further down the trotter following the bone; you should get down to the first *claws*! Now roll the skin down the trotter toward the nails until you come to the two nails sticking out to the side. Cut these at the joint so they stay part of your trotter skin, and ease the skin down a wee bit further to the main joint, before the *cloven hooves*! Give this joint a firm bend until it cracks, and finish splitting with a knife. The hooves stay on as they seal the end of the leg. Sprinkle the trotter skins with salt and put them in the fridge.

Pop the bones into a pot with your stock vegetables and herbs and cover with water. Bring to a boil and simmer for 2½ hours, skimming regularly. When done, strain the liquor, and discard the bones and vegetables.

Shake the salt off the trotters and lay them in a baking pan. Nestle in the cloves of garlic, and cover with a mixture of the pig's trotter stock and red wine. Cover with aluminum foil and place in a medium 350°F oven. Cook for approximately 3 hours, then check; it's cooked when your fingers easily meet if you pinch the trotter skin. You have to be careful at this point: you want your trotters well cooked but not collapsing! Leave to cool in the liquor, but remove before it has turned to jelly.

At this point you can put the trotters in the fridge if you have had enough for one day, but remember to bring them out in plenty of time before the final stage to warm up, as when cold they will not be so malleable.

Peel and cook your potatoes in salted water, until soft and ready for mashing. Drain, then mash them (or put through your food mill) without adding anything. Fry your shallots in a healthy spoonful of duck fat or olive oil, until soft but not brown. Mix these and the fat into your pure mashed potatoes and season with salt and pepper. Let this mixture cool to a handleable temperature. Fill your trotter skins with the mixture—not too full, as the potato will expand, but so they look like whole trotters again. Then wrap each trotter in a layer of caul fat, keeping this as thin as possible. At this point it is good to let the reconstructed trotters rest overnight in the fridge.

To cook the trotters, heat an ovenproof frying pan, add a spoonful of duck fat or olive oil, season the wrapped trotters with salt and pepper and brown them, being careful not to puncture the caul layer, then place them in a hot 425°F oven for 15 to 20 minutes. The caul should all but cook away, leaving a crispy trotter full of giving swollen mashed potatoes which have sopped up the sticky goodness of the trotter. Eat hot with watercress.

POTATOES

I am not an expert on American potato varieties, but ideally you are looking for a potato of a floury nature, not a waxy variety that will give you gluey mash.

CRISPY PIG'S TAILS

On other pages I have sung the praises of how the pig's snout and belly both have that special lip-sticking quality of fat and flesh merging, but this occurs in no part of the animal as wonderfully as on the tail. Like an ice cream on a stick, a pig's tail offers up all the above on a well-behaved set of bones. By the by, dealing with any slightly hairy extremities of pig, I recommend a throwaway Bic razor (hot towels and shaving cream *not required*). You must ask your butcher for long tails.

8 long pig's tails

2 onions, peeled and roughly chopped

2 carrots, peeled and roughly chopped

2 stalks of celery, chopped

a bundle of fresh herbs tied together

3 bay leaves

10 black peppercorns

1 head of garlic, skin on

zest of 1 lemon

½ bottle of red wine

1 quart chicken or light veal stock

2 tablespoons prepared English mustard

4 eggs, whisked together

3½ cups flour, seasoned with salt and peper

3 cups fresh fine white breadcrumbs

a large knob of unsalted butter

Place the tails in an ovenproof dish with the vegetables, herbs, bay leaves, peppercorns, garlic, lemon zest, and wine, and cover with the stock. Cover with aluminum foil, place in a medium 350°F oven, and cook for 3 hours, checking on the tails so they do not cook too fast; when done you should be able to easily pinch through the flesh. Remove from the oven. Allow to cool in the stock, but remove the tails before it turns to jelly and drain any excess liquid off them (you can refrigerate them at this point).

When the tails are cold and firm, mix together the mustard and eggs and have ready three bowls: flour, egg and mustard, and breadcrumbs. Dust them with flour, roll them in the egg and mustard mix, and finally coat them in the breadcrumbs so that they are well covered. (Do this just before you cook, otherwise the crumbs will go soggy.)

Get a large ovenproof frying pan or roasting pan hot, add the butter, and when sizzling add the tails and roll them around (watch out, they can and will spit—be very careful). Place in a hot 425°F oven for 10 minutes, then turn them over, making sure there is enough butter, and roast for another 10 minutes, keeping an eye on them so they do not burn.

Serve hot with watercress or red mustard salad (smallish salad leaves with reddish veins, a fiery kick, and a slightly hairy nature). Some may like a spot of malt or red wine vinegar on their tails. Encourage the use of fingers and much gnawing of the bone.

BOILED BELLY AND LENTILS

This dish celebrates the not quite meat, not quite fat, quality of pork belly. There's nothing like a pork belly to steady the nerves.

THE BOILED BELLY

4½-pound piece of pork belly with its skin and bones

2 carrots, peeled

2 onions, peeled and stuck with 8 cloves

2 leeks, cleaned

2 stalks of celery

2 heads of garlic, skin on

a bunch of fresh herbs tied together

black peppercorns

Boiled belly

Brine your piece of pork belly according to the instructions on page 76. Let it sit in the brine for a nice 10 days. Then remove and rinse it.

Place the pork belly in a pan with all the other ingredients, and cover with water. Bring to a boil, skim, reduce to a very gentle simmer with the water barely moving, and cook for 3½ hours, until the flesh is soft and giving, but not collapsing. Remove from the water, slice, and serve with lentils and mustard.

Encourage your dining companions to eat the fat and all. With the rich and fatty belly you want quite dour lentils.

PORK BELLY Pork belly is a wonderful thing. It's onomatopoeic, belly is like it sounds—reassuring, steadying, and splendid to cook due to its fatty nature. It's not a cut of meat to rush; with that, a certain calm is imbued in the belly.

THE LENTILS

extra-virgin olive oil

1 onion, peeled and chopped into thin slices

1 leek, cleaned and chopped into thin slices

5 cloves of garlic, peeled and finely chopped

2 carrots, peeled and chopped in half, then into ¼-inch-thick slices

1 pound (about 2½ cups) Puy lentils

a bundle of thyme and parsley tied together

sea salt and freshly ground black pepper

a big handful of chopped curly parsley

Lentils

Cover the bottom of a largish pan with olive oil, and sweat your chopped vegetables. At the moment they are only just starting to soften, not coloring, add the lentils. Stir these for a couple of minutes in the oil and vegetables, then cover with water and nestle in the thyme and parsley bundle. Simmer and stir occasionally—you want the lentils soft but not squidgy, so that they have reserved their lentil integrity, but are not still individual hard nuts. This should take about 40 minutes. If they dry out add a spot more water.

Now season, which, particularly with lentils, is a very exciting moment. It is amazing what simple salt and pepper do to the flavor of lentils— they make lentils of them. Just before serving, stir in your chopped parsley and a healthy splash of extra-virgin olive oil, which will enrich and give a shine to your lentils, as they can veer to the dull side.

MAKING A BRINE

You can use your brine to preserve many of the meats you will use in this book, e.g., pork belly, beef brisket, bottom round, or ox tongue. Some recommend saltpeter instead of sea salt; I always feel it is a little too ferocious, and as a result am aware of it at the eating stage.

2 cups superfine (caster) sugar (many suggest brown sugar, but not me)

2¼ cups coarse sea salt

12 juniper berries

12 cloves

12 black peppercorns

3 bay leaves

4 quarts water

Bring all the brine ingredients together in a pot, and bring to a boil so the sugar and salt melt. Decant into a container and allow to cool. When cold add your meat, and leave it in the brine for the number of days required for your recipe.

Even though the brine is a preserving process, we are celebrating its flavor-enhancing properties, so just in case in these somewhat bacterially anxious days it is probably no bad thing to keep your brine and its contents in the fridge.

SOME BRINY THOUGHTS

Your brine bucket (made of a non-corrodible substance), kept in the fridge, will become a nurtured friend, whose character should improve with time and should give delicious results. Think of a corned beef sandwich. Your bucket makes a very useful holding tank if you are trying to amass some of the less readily available piggy parts—ears or tails, for example.

BRINED PORK BELLY, ROASTED

A delicious and cheap cut of pig.

a brine (see page 76)

4½-pound piece of pork belly, with its rind and bones

2 onions, peeled and chopped

a minuscule splash of olive oil

a pinch of coarse sea salt

Brine your pork belly piece for 3 days, rinse, then score the rind gently with a sharp knife (a retractable blade knife is excellent for this purpose).

Place the onions on the bottom of a roasting pan (their purpose is, as well as flavor, to stop the belly sticking). Lay the belly on top. Rub the rind with a little oil and then the salt. Place in a medium to hot 375°F oven for 1½ to 2 hours; keep an eye on it so it does not burn. If you're anxious that the rind is not crisping up, you can start or finish the belly under the broiler.

When cooked you should have crispy rind on top of soft and giving fatty flesh. Lift off the onions and serve.

BEANS AND BACON

TO FEED FOUR, BUT CAN EASILY EXPAND AND IS A GOOD DISH FOR MANY HEARTY EATERS ON A COLD DAY,

SO GO AS BIG AS YOUR POT ALLOWS YOU

"Landlord, bring us beans and bacon and a bottle of your finest Burgundy." A whole head of garlic (unpeeled) added to a dish produces that sweet garlic flavor that expresses its sweet untampered nature.

2 pounds navy beans, soaked overnight

1 pig's trotter (see page 38); 2 quarts of chicken stock will be splendid if no trotter is available

2 carrots, peeled

2 whole onions, peeled, plus 3 onions peeled and chopped

2 stalks of celery

3 heads of garlic, unpeeled

a bundle of fresh herbs: thyme, rosemary, parsley tied together

2- to 2¼-pound (see page 79) piece of unsmoked streaky bacon, with rind on

duck fat or olive oil

2 leeks, trimmed and chopped

one 28-ounce can plum tomatoes

sea salt and freshly ground black pepper

Put the beans into a pan with clean unsalted water; bring to a boil, skim, reduce to a simmer, and cook until thoroughly giving. This will take approximately 1½ hours. As soon as they meet the salty bacon they will stop getting any softer, in fact they seem to firm up. (Many recipes suggest soaking and blanching for 10 minutes is enough, but in my experience, once they meet salt—however long you cook them for—they never give in.) Once cooked, remove from the heat, but keep them in their liquor.

Separately cover your trotter with water, add the carrots, whole onions, celery, 1 head of garlic, and the herbs, and bring to a boil. Skim, reduce to a simmer, and cook for 2½ hours.

While all this is happening, remove the rind from the piece of bacon, if possible in one piece, and slice the bacon into ⅜-inch-thick slices.

Get a deep pan hot, and add a healthy dollop of duck fat or oil. First fry the piece of bacon rind, fat down, so it releases some of its fat into the pan, and remove;

then color your bacon slices and remove; then fry your chopped onions and leeks until softened and add the tomatoes, crushing them with your hands as you do. Let this cook down for 20 minutes to sweeten the tomatoes, stirring to loosen all the good bits of bacon that might adhere to the pan, season with salt and pepper, remembering the bacon is salty, add 2 ladles of the trotter stock, and let cook for another 10 minutes. Drain the beans but keep their liquor, add the beans to the pan, and mix with the tomato base.

Now for the final construction. Find a thick pot with a lid that will fit all your ingredients. At the bottom of the pot lay your bacon rind, fat down, then a layer of your saucy beans, strips of bacon, beans, a nestled trotter and 2 heads of garlic, beans, bacon, beans, and so on . . .

When everything is in place, top up with trotter stock to just cover the beans (if this runs out, use the bean juice or chicken stock). Cover and put in a medium to hot 375°F oven for 1½ hours, then uncover and cook for a further 30 minutes until a crustiness forms on the top. Serve hot from the pot on the table with much red wine.

BACON You have two varieties of this splendid thing in its many shapes and forms: salted only (unsmoked), and salted and smoked. Almost every cut of the pig lends itself to these processes, and in the results hang limitless possibilities: fried with eggs; a hock added to a dish of beans; chunks of bacon as a fine companion to other meats slowly braised. Even the rind is a fine addition to many a dish, bringing fat and flavor to the party. Streaky bacon is much like its American cousin, only leaner.

PIG'S CHEEK AND TONGUE

TO FEED TWO

a brine (see page 76)

1 pig's head

stock vegetables (carrots, leeks, onion, celery; see page 3)

a bundle of herbs tied together

black peppercorns

a splash of red wine vinegar

Brine your pig's head for 3 days, rinse it, and place it in a large pot with the stock vegetables, herbs, peppercorns, and vinegar. Cover with water and bring to a boil. Reduce to a gentle simmer and cook for 2½ to 3 hours. The cheeks should come away easily from the skull; keep these warm in the broth. Open the pig's jaw and pull out the tongue. Peel it while still warm and slice in half lengthwise, so each diner gets a cheek and half a tongue. Serve with mashed potatoes and Green Sauce (page 164).

BATH CHAPS Bath chaps are a specialty of the West Country (England), and if you have a spirited butcher he may prepare them for you wherever you are, if asked nicely. They are a boned-out pig's head, which is rolled so the tongue is in the center, surrounded by the cheeks and their protective layer of fat, and tapering to one end where you have the snout. This should then be brined for 3 days, and boiled in a similar fashion to the whole head (page 39), though 2 hours' cooking time should be ample, not having the skull to contend with. You can then slice it and serve it hot with mashed potatoes and Green Sauce, as with the Pig's Cheek and Tongue (above); or allow it to go cold, slice it thinly, and eat it with gherkins; or fry slices, which are delicious if served with greens tossed in a mustard dressing (page 170).

ROAST PORK LOIN, TURNIPS, GARLIC, AND ANCHOVIES

TO SERVE SIX

Is it not splendid when you have a guest to stay who cooks delicious things for you? A fine example is Ken, a chef from Sydney, who prepared this splendid dish full of most of my favorite things. He even finished it off with a healthy splash of truffle oil, which I have omitted from this version, but please express yourself.

about 5½ pounds pork loin on the bone (you will want six chops out of it at the end): ask the butcher to leave the skin on, chine it but *not* score it

2 onions, peeled and chopped

sea salt and freshly ground black pepper

18 cloves of garlic with skin on, separated, roasted in the oven until soft and sweet, then squeezed out of their skins and mashed

1 small can anchovies in oil, drained and finely chopped

a handful of capers (extra-fine if possible)

a handful of curly parsley, chopped

a healthy splash of extra-virgin olive oil

a splash of red wine vinegar

12 small or 6 large turnips, peeled and chopped, greens reserved; rocket (arugula) makes a good substitute for the greens

Remove the skin of the pork in one piece (this is not hard: with a thin, sharp knife, gently slice under the skin, following it around the pork), then gently score it (if in doubt your butcher will remove the bone and score it for you). Place the skin back where it was before. In a roasting pan lay out your onions and place your pork and skin on top of them, then season with salt and pepper. Put into a hot 425°F oven for 2½ hours.

Meanwhile, make your dressing: mix the garlic, anchovies, capers, parsley, oil, vinegar, and pepper, and keep at the ready. Fifteen minutes before the pork is done, cook your turnips in boiling salted water. When cooked add the greens, then drain straightaway. Place these into a serving bowl, dress, and toss so all get to know the dressing. Remove the pork from the oven; it will hold its heat well and will enjoy a rest if things are a little out of sync.

If the skin is not crispy enough return it to the oven to crisp up while you slice the loin into chops. Place these on top of the dressed turnips and greens. Finally, remove the crisp skin from the oven and roughly chop it with a big knife. Top the dish off with this and serve.

POT ROAST BRISKET

Both this and the Boiled Beef and Dumplings recipe (page 84) provide very good leftovers for your hash, or are excellent in sandwiches, or simply cold, thinly sliced, with Green Sauce (page 164) or Horseradish Sauce (page 166). You can salt the brisket yourself for 5 days in a brine (page 76) or if you don't want to make it yourself, you can buy corned brisket from the butcher.

2 carrots, peeled and chopped

3 onions, peeled and chopped

2 leeks cleaned, trimmed and chopped

2 whole heads of garlic, skin on

a bundle of fresh herbs tied together

10 black peppercorns

4½-pound piece of brisket of beef

1 quart unsalted chicken stock

2 cups red wine

In a deep roasting pan, just a bit bigger than your beef, lay your chopped vegetables, garlic, herbs, and peppercorns, onto which nestle your brisket. Pour the stock and wine over it. You are looking for an iceberg effect: part of the beef is not covered but we know there is a lot more submerged in the stock. Cover with aluminum foil. Put into a medium 350°F oven for 3 hours, until thoroughly giving but not collapsing (keep an eye on it; do not let it cook too fast, and turn the oven down if this is the case).

Then slice and eat it, ladling a little of the juice over the meat (keep the remaining juice, which makes a very good base for soup). Serve with Horseradish Sauce.

HASH

A very good dish if you are feeling a little dented.

This is a useful and delicious way of using up the remains of your Pot Roast Brisket (page 82) and Boiled Beef and Dumplings (page 84). I cannot tell how much you will have left over, so we cannot be exact here. Look at your remains and decide what will be appropriate. You will need roughly equal amounts of meat and veg.

leftover brisket

onions, peeled and chopped

oil

canned plum tomatoes

potatoes, peeled, boiled, and chopped

sea salt

freshly ground black pepper

1 free-range egg per person

Shred your cold brisket, and keep to one side. Fry the onions in oil until soft, crush a few plum tomatoes into the pan, and let these cook down. Add the potatoes and beef and season with salt and pepper. Keep tossing in the pan until it's all heated through; if it's getting dry add some juice from the canned tomatoes, but it is good if the potatoes get a bit of color. Serve with a fried egg on top.

BOILED BEEF AND DUMPLINGS

Another dish for which you have to think ahead and get your beef in a brine for 12 days. Make sure your butcher does not roll and tie your beef. At the end of 12 days rinse and soak the beef thoroughly.

This is the true John Bull feast served with Horseradish Sauce (page 166) and pickled walnuts. I am not being jingoistic in including this dish; once you have amassed the beef, dumpling, horseradish, and pickled walnut on your fork, it is a heady combination, bigger than our borders.

5½ pounds brisket or bottom round, brined (page 76) for 12 days, then soaked and rinsed

a bundle of parsley and thyme tied together

3 stalks of celery, chopped

2 bay leaves

10 black peppercorns

6 onions, peeled

6 carrots, peeled

6 leeks, cleaned

DUMPLINGS

¼ pound suet

1¾ cups self-rising flour

a pinch of sea salt and black pepper

1 beaten free-range egg

Place your beef in a pot (remember it has to be big enough to accommodate the vegetables as well), cover with water, and add your herb bundle, celery, bay leaves, and peppercorns. Bring up to a boil, skim, reduce to a very gentle simmer, with barely signs of movement in the water, and cook for approximately 4 hours. Prod with a knife to check how the meat feels— it should be giving, but not collapsing! After the meat has been simmering for 2 hours put in the onions; ½ hour after adding the onions, add the carrots; and after a further ½ hour add the leeks. Keep an eye on your vegetables so they do not overcook—you can always remove them. However, this is a dish that demands well-cooked vegetables, no al dente here.

When everything is ready, remove the meat and vegetables to a serving dish and keep them warm, with a splash of broth to moisten. Make the dumplings as follows.

Bring the broth to a bubbling simmer. Meanwhile, mix the dumpling ingredients together, adding some cold water: you are looking for quite a sticky dough. Shape into walnut-sized balls and drop into your simmering broth—they should take about 10 minutes to cook, and should be like little suet clouds.

The boiled beef also goes with Aïoli (page 162) or Green Sauce (page 164). If you accompany your beef with either of these, do not include the dumplings, pickled walnuts, or horseradish.

PICKLED WALNUTS

are walnuts that are pickled while they still have their green skin, before the shell has begun to form within. They end up as delicious black, noduley orbs. I crave them so much sometimes I wonder if I'm pregnant.

BOILED OX TONGUE

You can salt the tongue yourself in a brine (page 76); keep the tongue in it for 7 days. Alternatively, get a corned beef tongue from the butcher.

1 corned ox tongue, rinsed
  (see headnote)

2 carrots, peeled

2 leeks, cleaned

2 onions, peeled

1 head of garlic, skin on

10 black peppercorns

2 stalks of celery

a bunch of fresh herbs tied
  together

Cover all the ingredients with water in a pot, bring gently to a boil, then reduce to the calmest of simmers and cook for 3½ hours. When the tongue is cooked its skin will peel away easily; also check its givingness by stabbing it with a thin, sharp knife. Peel while still warm, as this is much easier. Tongue is a very dexterous element in a dish, and has many friends: serve it hot or cold, broiled or fried, in a sandwich with English mustard and tomato, with a caper sauce, or with Horseradish or Green Sauce (pages 166 and 164), and it is particularly good with beets, for example in Tongue and Beets (page 87).

TONGUE AND BEETS

4 pounds fresh beets, whole, skin on

2 cups water

2 splashes of extra-virgin olive oil

sea salt and freshly ground black pepper

a splash of balsamic vinegar

1 cold cooked tongue (page 86)

Horseradish Sauce (page 166)

In a deep roasting pan, place the beets, water, a splash of olive oil, salt, and pepper. Cover with aluminum foil and place in a hot 450°F oven for approximately 45 minutes. Check by stabbing the beets with a knife. Once they are done, peel the beets while hot (kitchen gloves help in this task) and cut into merry chunks. Dress the beets with oil, balsamic vinegar, salt, and pepper. Serve with a thin slice of cold tongue (the beets start to warm the cold tongue, loosening it) and Horseradish Sauce.

TRIPE AND ONIONS

Do not let the word tripe deter you, let its soothing charms win you over and enjoy it as do those who always have! Visually, as well as gastronomically, there is a great serenity to a plate of tripe and onions.

1 quart milk

3 onions, peeled and roughly chopped

a healthy pinch of mace

4¼ to 4½ pounds white honeycomb tripe (which comes from the second stomach, the reticulum, of the ox), cut into 1½ by 4½-inch strips

sea salt and freshly ground black pepper

¾ cup unsalted butter

1½ cups all-purpose flour

In a pot large enough to fit all the ingredients place the milk, onions, and mace. Bring to a boil, reduce to a simmer, and cook for 20 minutes.

Then add the tripe and season cautiously with salt and pepper (you can add more later). Bring up to a gentle boil, reduce again to a simmer, and cook for a further 45 minutes to 1 hour, checking the tripe's giving qualities with a sharp knife. Be careful, as if cooked too long tripe will just melt away.

Now, in another pan, melt the butter and add the flour. Cook this, stirring to avoid browning, until it smells biscuity. Continue stirring vigorously (a whisk might be useful here) and add a couple of ladles of the liquor from the tripe pot. Once thoroughly mixed and smooth, return this mixture to the tripe. Stir in thoroughly and simmer for a further 15 minutes to allow the dish to thicken slightly. Adjust the seasoning to taste and serve hot, using a slotted spoon, with mashed potatoes.

GRATIN OF TRIPE

Follow the previous recipe to its conclusion except instead of serving the tripe and onions with mashed potatoes, decant the tripe and its sauce into 4 ovenproof dishes (I think this is the only time I recommend individual dishes, but this recipe works well this way and everyone loves their own little gratin). Cover with a layer of fine white breadcrumbs made with yesterday's bread, dot with little knobs of butter, and place the dishes in a very hot oven until the tripe liquor is bubbling away. If the crust has not browned at this point, stick the dishes under the broiler. When the dishes are golden brown they are ready to serve.

The eaters will each need a spoon as well as the usual tools. Advise them to stick their napkins in their collars to protect their fronts as, unlike Tripe and Onions, which is given structure by mashed potatoes, so helping the journey from the plate to the mouth, tripe gratinéed, without this structural aid, is very sloppy.

TRIPE Tripe is generally from the ox's stomach. It comes in various thicknesses and colors. The most readily available tripe in Britain and the U.S. is the bleached honeycomb variety; hence the recipes in this book are geared toward this variety. On behalf of all tripe, *tripe is great* and don't hesitate to welcome it into your gastronomic life.

HAGGIS

You will need a meat grinder.

1 sheep's stomach (see note page 91)

1 sheep's pluck, which should include the heart, lights (lungs), windpipe, liver, and some intestines

sea salt

3 onions, peeled and chopped

a knob of unsalted butter

2¼ cups pinhead oatmeal (see note, page 91), toasted (if not, bake in a flat pan in a hot oven, but don't burn or brown it)

6 ounces prepared suet

2 cups of the water the pluck was cooked in, or 2 cups chicken stock

freshly ground black pepper

ground allspice

Wash the stomach in cold water then leave to soak. Thoroughly rinse the pluck and lights (lungs) in cold running water. Do not be put off by the initial look of your ingredients. Place the pluck in a large pot, and cover with generously salted water. The pluck should have the windpipe attached and you should hang this over the edge of your pan, with a pot underneath to catch anything the lungs may expel while cooking. Bring to a boil, then reduce to a simmer and cook for 2 hours, regularly skimming. Allow to cool in the liquor. Once the pluck is cold, remove it from its water and reserve 2 cups of it; cut the windpipe off, if present, and discard it. Cut the pluck into pieces, then coarsely mince in a meat grinder. If the pluck did not have its windpipe, the water you have cooked the pluck in is less tempting to use to moisten your haggis in the later stages, so use the suggested alternative of chicken stock.

Meanwhile, fry the onions in butter until soft and if the oatmeal is untoasted toast it now.

Mix into the meat the oatmeal, suet, and onions, watching the consistency, and add the cooking liquor, or chicken stock if the former is not looking too inviting. Season with salt, and particularly with pepper and allspice, and taste.

Find part of the stomach (make sure the textural side is turned inward) with no holes in it. Stuff this with the mixture, and tie tightly at either end, leaving plenty of extra stomach at the outer side of the knot (when trimming off the rest of the stomach), to allow for movement. Do not be alarmed that this does not look like any haggis you have ever seen, and that the stomach bag looks too thick, all will be well. Wrap in aluminum foil with a little kink in it to allow for expansion, which will take place. Cook for 3 hours in gently simmering water.

To serve, remove from the water and foil, slice it open, and spoon it out. Eat with mashed rutabagas and mashed potatoes. In honor of the Auld Alliance, I find that Dijon mustard goes very well with haggis.

Notes

Sheep's stomach is the sack that will become the casing for the haggis.

Sheep's pluck is like a diagram of the animal's organs all still attached. *Lights* is another word for lungs.

Pinhead oatmeal is exactly as it sounds; rather than rolled oats or finely ground oatmeal, it resembles the sturdy end of a pin. Irish oatmeal is available this way.

HAGGIS

Having made a plea to the readers of this book to tuck into tripe a few pages previously, I must point out that particularly on Robert Burns Night (January 25), no one seems to have any qualms about sitting down to a feast of haggis. This is possibly due to folk not knowing what goes into a haggis. My belief is that it's more a matter of geometry—the reassuring rounded form, like a large sausage, is territory everyone seems to feel safe with. As dishes go this is quite involved, but the satisfaction of sitting down to your own haggis and raising a dram!

KID AND FENNEL

The lady who supplies much of our goat cheese has to slaughter a certain number of the young goats (kids) each year to keep her herd within manageable numbers, much to our delight, as the flesh is delicious, having youth on its side.

One hind leg of kid will vary in size and can feed from two to three to sometimes four. I have to leave you to judge your leg and your appetite.

a splash of olive oil

1 leg of kid

3 bulbs of fennel, cut against the grain into ½-inch slices

12 shallots, peeled and left whole

12 cloves of garlic, peeled and left whole

a bundle of fresh thyme, rosemary, and parsley (herbs you can imagine the young kid skipping through) tied together

sea salt and freshly ground black pepper

½ cup Pernod

1 cup white wine

2½ cups chicken stock

a splash of extra-virgin olive oil

In a heated frying pan drop a splash of olive oil and brown the leg of kid, then place it in an ovenproof dish or roasting pan. Sweat the vegetables in the frying pan (do not color them), then place these around the leg of kid, add the herb bundle, seasoning, Pernod, wine, and chicken stock, and a splash of extra-virgin olive oil— the liquid does not have to cover everything. Cover with aluminum foil and place in a hot 425°F oven for 20 minutes, then turn down to medium 350°F for approximately another 2 hours; halfway through turn your leg over. Check with a knife that the leg and vegetables are cooked; if they're ready, slice the leg, and with a slotted spoon put the vegetables in a bowl. Pour the remaining juice into a jug and serve all three together.

LAMB AND BARLEY STEW

A dish which likes to be made a day before eating.

5½ pounds lamb: shoulder and neck chops are appropriate; keep them on the bone and ask your butcher to chop them into appropriate pieces

a bundle of thyme, parsley, and 2 stalks of celery tied together

3 bay leaves

10 black peppercorns

sea salt

8 small carrots, peeled, or 2 big carrots, peeled and chopped in quarters

16 shallots, peeled

4 kohlrabies, peeled and cut in half

8 leeks, trimmed and cleaned

a good handful (or small cup) of barley; this may not seem much but it expands and has a habit of taking over

Place the lamb, herb bundle, bay leaves, peppercorns, and a pinch of salt in a pan, cover with water, bring to a boil, skim, reduce to the gentlest of simmers, and add the vegetables and barley. Cook for 1 hour. Check the meat with a knife to see if it is giving, but catch it before it is overcooked (watch that it never cooks too fast). Decant into a clean china container and allow to cool in its broth. When cold a layer of fat should form on the surface; remove this. When it's time to eat, return the lamb, vegetables, barley, and broth to a pan, bring up to a boil, and reduce to a simmer until all is hot. Check the seasoning and remove the thyme bundle. Serve on deepish plates so the broth can be enjoyed as well.

Some may be tempted to add more *oomph* to this dish, but I'm all for its soothing, gentle qualities.

LAMB'S TONGUES, TURNIPS, AND BACON

TO SERVE FOUR

6 lamb's tongues (give them a
    rinse with cold water)

7 cups chicken stock

1 head of garlic, separated
    and peeled

a bundle of fresh thyme and
    parsley tied together

6 young turnips with healthy
    greens chopped off but
    kept (if no greens, rocket
    [arugula] makes a good
    substitute, or if you want
    something with more
    body, curly kale is delicious
    in this dish)

2 dollops of duck fat or
    unsalted butter

16 shallots, peeled and left
    whole

1¼ pound piece of smoked
    streaky bacon (see
    page 79), skinned and
    cut into chunks

sea salt and freshly ground
    black pepper

sherry vinegar or red wine
    vinegar

Step one

In a pot cover the lamb's tongues with the chicken stock. Add the garlic and herbs, bring to a boil, then reduce to a gentle simmer and cook for approximately 2 hours, until the tongues are giving. Remove the tongues and allow to cool, just to a handleable temperature, then peel, as they are much easier to peel when warm. While doing this cook your turnips in the stock.

When cooked remove the turnips from the stock, take it off the heat, and return the peeled tongues to the cooling stock.

Step two

In an ovenproof frying pan, melt the duck fat or butter
and fry the shallots just enough to color them, not
burn them. Then pop them into a medium to hot
375°F oven to roast for 15 minutes, again watching
that they do not burn. When soft, sweet, and giving,
remove them from the oven. Now remove the tongues
from the stock and slice them in half lengthwise. Heat
a deep frying pan that has a lid, or a shallow saucepan.
Melt a spot of duck fat, fry the bacon in this so as to
slightly color it, add the tongue and turnips, allow
these to color, then add the shallots and a healthy
splash of the stock to half-cover the pan's contents. Let
this start to boil, add the greens and season with salt
and pepper, then cover the pan and turn the heat down
to a simmer and cook for 2 minutes. With a slotted
spoon remove the ingredients to a hot deep plate, then
ladle some of the liquor in the pan over, making it as
dry or as brothy as you wish. Just before eating
sprinkle the dish with a little vinegar.

Just as delicious, if not more so, is to substitute fava
beans for the turnips (these do not need to be cooked
before the final stage). You still need the rocket or kale,
as the greens act as a structural weave in the dish.

STUFFED LAMB'S HEARTS

STUFFING

duck fat or unsalted butter

4 red onions, peeled and
sliced

4 cloves of garlic, peeled and
chopped

2 cups red wine

½ pound yesterday's white
bread, with crusts off,
cubed

sea salt and freshly ground
black pepper

half a bunch of sage, leaves
only, chopped

LAMB'S HEARTS

6 lamb's hearts (make sure
they are intact, with a hole
only at the top)

18 rashers (slices) of smoked
streaky bacon (see page 79)

4½ cups chicken stock

First make the stuffing. In a pan with duck fat or butter cook your onions and garlic gently so that they do not color but become soft and giving. Add the wine, let this reduce by half, then add the bread, season with salt and pepper, and cook together gently for 15 minutes; you want the stuffing to have an *unctuous* but not squidgy quality, so if it appears too dry add a splash more wine. Let the stuffing cool, then add the sage.

Meanwhile trim the hearts of any excess fat nodules at their openings and any obvious sinews, and the flap at the top that looks like the bit that has a string to tighten at the top of a knapsack. Finally, with your finger, scoop out any blood clots at the base of the ventricles. You are ready to stuff.

With your hand, press the stuffing into the heart, and level off the opening at the top. Then drape 3 rashers of bacon over the exposed stuffing in a star fashion, forming a lid, and secure with string.

Find an ovenproof dish or deep roasting pan in which the hearts will fit snugly, and stand them upright. Pour stock over them. They do not need to be completely covered but almost is good. Cover with aluminum foil and place in a medium 350°F oven for 2½ hours. When cooked remove the hearts and keep them warm. Strain the juice and then quickly reduce by half for a delicious sauce. Untie the hearts and serve with mashed rutabaga.

DEVILED KIDNEYS

The perfect breakfast on your birthday, with a glass of Black Velvet (half Guinness and half Champagne).

6 lamb's kidneys, suet and membrane removed, and slit in half lengthwise to retain the kidney shape

3 tablespoon all-purpose flour

1 teaspoon cayenne pepper or to taste

1 teaspoon Coleman's Dry English Mustard Powder

sea salt and freshly ground black pepper

a big knob of unsalted butter

Worcestershire sauce

a healthy splash of chicken stock

2 pieces of toast (white or brown, up to you, though—just an observation—white seems to sop up the juices better)

Nip out the white fatty gristle of the kidneys with a knife or scissors. Mix together the flour, cayenne pepper, mustard, salt, and pepper in a bowl.

Get a frying pan very hot, throw in a knob of butter, and as this melts roll your kidneys in your spiced flour, then shake them in a sieve to remove the excess. Place them in the sizzling pan, cook for 2 minutes each side, add a hearty splash of Worcestershire and the chicken stock, and let all the ingredients get to know each other. Remove the kidneys to your two waiting bits of toast, let the sauce reduce and emulsify in the pan (do not let it disappear) and pour over the kidneys and toast. Eat. Happy Birthday!

RENDERING AND PRESERVING IN FAT

Traditionally, Britain being a seafaring nation, preserving food has always been important; unfortunately, the home freezer has eclipsed another method that bears delicious results: the process of rendering, cooking, and preserving in fat, which produces tender, flavorsome meat that keeps, improving with age, and could not be more versatile in its gastronomic possibilities.

In the sixteenth century, for long sea journeys, cooked ducks and mallards were preserved in their own fat, butter, and spices. In France the practice of confit (cooking and preserving meat in fat) has remained fundamental in modern kitchens. In Britain potting meat (cooking meat, shredding it, and covering it with an air-tight layer of butter or suet) is still popular. But in a country full of ducks and geese, why are we not using the fat like the sixteenth-century navy?

Ducks and geese are extraordinary fat providers. Put your hand into their cavity and you should be able to pull out a great clump of fat; place this in a pan and heat to a melting simmer. When it appears all the fat has flown, strain it into a jar, seal it and allow it to cool, then refrigerate. Using the same method you can also render down pork fat. Roast a duck and see how fat collects in your roasting pan. Again, pour this off into a jar, seal it, allow it to cool, then refrigerate. If you still need more fat you can always buy cans or jars of duck or goose fat.

HOW TO DO IT

In a plastic, glass, or china container, scantily scatter coarse sea salt, crushed peppercorns, and twigs of thyme. Place a layer of your chosen uncooked meat and repeat your scattering. Keep on with this layering until done. Cover and leave in the fridge for 24 hours. This, as well as flavoring it, removes water from the meat.

The next day there should be a salty puddle at the base of your container. Remove the meat, and vigorously brush off any remaining salt, pepper, and thyme. Dry the meat with a clean kitchen towel, place in an ovenproof dish or pan, cover with duck, goose, or pork fat, or a combination, then cover with foil.

Cook in a medium 325°F to 350°F oven until the flesh is giving; check with a sharp knife, but avoid the falling apart (approximate cooking times for the various ingredients are given on page 99). When it's cooked, remove the meat to a glass, plastic, or china container that you can seal, then pour fat over to cover. Seal the container, allow it to cool, and refrigerate. The only exception to this is the tongue which, while warm, should be peeled, then returned to the fat. This will now keep and improve for many months.

WHAT TO DO WITH YOUR GOODIES IN FAT

After being gently cooked immersed in fat, the meat is flavorsome, giving, and amazingly versatile. Duck, goose, or rabbit legs are a meal in themselves when heated in a hot oven so that the skin can crisp up, or sorted through and shredded in a salad. So, too, with the giblets: use them warmed in a salad, in a terrine such as the Duck Neck Terrine (page 50), in stews—the possibilities hold no bounds. If cooking a lentil or bean stew the confit of pork belly or skin could not be anywhere happier. Eat the tongues (at room temperature so the fat can run off) sliced with pickles or mixed into a salad, pan-fry slices, or make a kind of rich pressed tongue by placing the warm tongue into a terrine or loaf pan lined with plastic wrap, drizzling over some of the fat, and putting under great pressure.

The fantastic thing is you can then reuse the fat for preserving or cooking with. So as you can see, restaurants are confiting madly, and so should you at home.

APPROXIMATE COOKING TIMES IN FAT	
Duck legs	2¼ hours
Goose legs	2¾ hours
Duck or goose gizzards, necks, hearts	2 hours
Rabbit's legs	2 hours
Lamb's tongues	2 hours
Pig's tongues	2½ hours
Pork belly	2½ hours
Pork skin	1½ hours

KEEPING TIMES

Food preserved in fat has fantastic longevity, if kept in the fridge and properly covered in fat, but nature being nature there is now and then a batch that does not wish to grow old gracefully. So this method of preserving is not forever, and I recommend using within six months.

LAMB'S KIDNEYS IN THEIR SUET

Lamb's kidneys still in their suet should not be a problem for your butcher to arrange. If there are large amounts of suet, trim it down but try not to expose the actual kidney. I think two kidneys per person.

2 lamb's kidneys

the merest gesture of olive oil

sea salt and freshly ground
  black pepper

Get an ovenproof frying pan very hot, add oil, and season your kidneys thoroughly, especially with salt. Place them in the pan, brown them all over, and place the whole thing in a hot 425°F oven for 8 minutes. Remove the kidneys from the oven and from the pan, which should be quite full of fat by now, leave them to rest somewhere warm for 4 to 5 minutes, then slice each one into four pieces. You should have the salty, crispy outside of the suet, melting rich fat within, and finally in the middle, the beautiful, blushing kidney. Serve hot with a watercress salad.

LAMB SHANKS EBEN'S WAY

Eben, an old friend of Margot's, uses a leg of lamb, but it is the fatty qualities of the lamb shank I have found to be most suited to this dish. This dish goes very well with quince cheese (a very firm paste which gets made from cooking down quinces and their natural pectin), a conserve you can get from delicatessens, village fêtes, and some supermarkets.

4 rear lamb shanks (if front shanks allow 2 per person)

20 raisins

4 cloves of garlic, peeled, each one sliced into 5 pieces

¼ cup red wine vinegar

4 cups red wine

4 juniper berries

4 whole allspice

10 black peppercorns

3 bay leaves

sea salt

1 cup port

Make 5 incisions into your lamb shanks, into each of which press a raisin and a slice of garlic. In a plastic or china container place the lamb shanks and all the other ingredients except the salt and port. Marinate for at least 2 days (they will not be covered—do not worry), turning the shanks every half day or so.

You will need a heavy pan with a well-fitting lid (not aluminum, because of the vinegar). Place the shanks and marinade in it, adding a healthy pinch of salt. Cover and place in a gentle to medium 325°F oven, and cook for approximately 3 hours, turning the shanks every 30 minutes. If they are cooking too fast, turn the oven down: the secret is slow and low with this dish. The shanks want to be thoroughly giving, but still just holding on to the bone. When this is achieved, remove the shanks and keep warm. Add the port to the juice, place it on the heat, and reduce until your sauce is to your satisfaction, skimming off the fat. Pour it over the shanks through a sieve (to remove the spices) and serve.

MUTTON AND BEANS

Unfortunately it's not easy these days to get your hands on mutton, which seems odd, as not that long ago a mutton chop was fundamental in the British diet; almost no formal meal went by without its appearing somewhere. However, persistence and a good butcher should suffice.

1 pound dried borlotti (cranberry) beans, soaked overnight and drained (they have a certain nuttiness)

1 leg of mutton

sea salt and freshly ground black pepper

unsalted butter

2¾-pound piece of unsmoked streaky bacon cut into chunks, rind removed and reserved (see page 79)

2 carrots, peeled and chopped

3 onions, peeled and chopped

3 leeks, cleaned and chopped

18 cloves of garlic, peeled and left whole

a bundle of fresh herbs tied together

4 bay leaves

½ bottle of red wine

1¾ quarts chicken stock

Cover your borlotti beans with clean water and cook for 1¼ hours. Check them—you want them cooked but not falling apart. Remove from the heat and drain, but keep the liquor.

Meanwhile season your mutton with salt and pepper, get a frying pan hot, add a large knob of butter, and allow it to sizzle. Reduce the heat slightly, and brown the leg of mutton in the pan. You want this to be a gentle buttery moment, not a ferocious burning moment.

Remove the mutton to an ovenproof dish or deep roasting pan large enough to hold all the ingredients. Brown the bacon and bacon rind in same frying pan, then add to the mutton. Gently cook the vegetables and garlic (if the pan seems too dry add a bit more butter), and then add these to the mutton and bacon, and nestle the herb bundle in. Also add the cooked borlotti beans and bay leaves, season with salt and pepper, and add the wine and stock. The contents of the dish, except the mutton, should be just covered; if this is not the case add some of the bean liquor. Cover with aluminum foil, place in a gentle to medium 325°F oven for 4 hours, turning the leg over every 40 minutes, and checking at about 3 hours with a knife. When it's ready, check the seasoning, cut chunks of giving mutton from the bone, and serve in deep plates with beans, vegetables, bacon, and juices.

BIRDS
AND
GAME

ROAST PIGEON AND OTHER GAME BIRDS

ALLOW 1 PIGEON PER PERSON

Pigeons (squab) are wonderful when cooked properly. Maybe they're not quite as delicious as more glamorous game birds, grouse, grey-legged partridge, or woodcock, but they're much cheaper and available almost all the year round. Do not be put off by the urban pigeon, think woods, countryside, and plump, cooing pigeons in trees.

pigeons, as many as you want

sea salt and freshly ground
    black pepper

a sprig of sage per pigeon

2 knobs of unsalted butter
    per pigeon

Season the pigeons inside and out with salt and pepper and stick the sage into the cavity with a walnut-sized knob of butter. Get an ovenproof frying pan hot, and melt another knob of butter; when sizzling, brown your pigeon in the pan, being careful not to leave the pigeon breast down against the hot pan for too long, as this is the most delicate part.

Right your pigeon so it's breast up, and place in a very hot 475°F oven for 8 to 10 minutes. When the butter inside the pigeon has melted it's a good indication that it's ready. Remove from the oven and place upside down on a warm plate somewhere warm but not so hot as to carry on cooking the bird (this allows the butter to seep into the breasts and moisten them), and leave to rest for 10 minutes, by which time the breasts will be a blushing red (in game birds, you more often than not look for a blush of red when you cut into their breasts). Serve with a sharp knife.

Other game birds

As for other game birds, I would apply the same cooking principle, allowing a couple more minutes for larger birds. The exceptions are your partridge, which should have the faintest of blushing breasts unlike the darker-fleshed birds, and the woodcock (page 107).

BIRDS AND GAME

105

ROAST QUAIL

The quail unfortunately falls into a kind of bird purgatory; it is not a game bird, though some describe it as such, but is now a thoroughly farmed bird, so not glamorous enough to warrant the "hands on" battling that people feel justified to exert on grouse and partridge, and is denied from joining the chicken's gang, as it is seen to be too fiddly to eat. Then finally, to kick the quail while it's down, people say it has no flavor.

Put all this behind you and let me put forward the case for the joys of a bowl of thoroughly roasted quails.

sea salt

freshly ground black pepper

10 quails (as there are always those who end up eating 3)

olive oil

Season the quails inside and out very thoroughly, being especially heavy on the salt. In a hot frying pan, with a small splash of olive oil, brown the quails all over. When you are satisfied with their color place them on a lightly oiled roasting pan and place in a hot 425°F oven for 20 minutes or so.

Despite the quail's fragile reputation it is robust when it comes to cooking, not having the drying out potential of the partridge or the angst of getting that perfect moment of blush in a grouse breast. The quail wants plenty of cooking, to the point that its legs can be pulled easily from the ribcage, and the flesh sucked off the leg bone. Serve the quail salty and well done in a bowl in the middle of the table and encourage some hands-on eating.

Serve with a bowl of lentils or simply a watercress salad.

ROAST WOODCOCK

1 woodcock, head removed
  but saved, per person

sea salt and freshly ground
  black pepper

unsalted butter

a splash of chicken stock (or
  gamebird stock, if you've
  got)

1 piece of toast per person

Woodcock defecate before they fly, so they can be roasted with the guts in, which heightens the flavor. Allow the same roasting and resting time as the pigeon (page 105), then, with a teaspoon, scoop out its guts into a hot frying pan with a knob of butter, allow to sizzle for a few moments, then rescue the liver with a spoon, and mix the ingredients remaining in the pan with a splash of stock, using the back of a spoon to work everything together.

Rest your woodcock on a piece of toast, onto which you have spread its liver, and pour the pan juices through a sieve over the bird. The head you also roast, wrapped in aluminum foil, and split open when serving, exposing its delicious brains: you will need a teaspoon for this. Unfortunately woodcock are not as plentiful as pigeons and are much more expensive, but they are worth it. They are one of the finest eating experiences.

PIGEON, CHICKPEAS, AND SPRING ONION

This is not really a recipe, more of a suggestion to bring together three basic, but very suited textures and flavors.

1 pound dried chickpeas, soaked overnight and drained

1 head of garlic, skin on, plus 4 cloves of garlic, peeled

1 tablespoon tahini

juice of 1 lemon

1¼ cups extra-virgin olive oil

a splash of Tabasco or more to taste

sea salt and freshly ground black pepper

4 pigeons

2 bunches of spring onions or scallions, washed and trimmed

Place your chickpeas in fresh clean water with the whole garlic and bring to a boil, then simmer for approximately 2 hours, until cooked. Drain (keep the chickpea water, as it makes a very good vegetarian stock), put half the cooked chickpeas into the food processor with the tahini and peeled garlic, whizz, and add the lemon juice and some of the oil: you are looking for a loose-ish consistency, not a thick glump. Add the Tabasco, salt and pepper, and the rest of the chickpeas, then whizz again, but keeping these coarser—coarse is good here.

Roast the pigeons as on page 105, allow them to cool to a warm and handleable temperature, then with a sharp knife remove the breasts and legs by following the bird's back- and breastbone down its carcass.

Serve with the chickpea purée still slightly warm and a bowl of spring onions. You have got the gamey meat, the soothing, nutty chickpeas, and the stimulating *gnya* of the spring onions.

GIBLET STEW

When on the menu at St. John this dish's name has been known to cause some small surprise among our diners, but when tried it has won over the most skeptical, for it is simply wonderful.

1 cup white haricot (navy) beans (this is enough for the beans to be emphatically present, yet the dish is not too beany), soaked overnight and drained

2 heads of garlic, skin on, cut in half

6 duck necks, preserved in duck fat (see page 98)

6 duck hearts, preserved in duck fat

6 duck gizzards (once trimmed become 2 halves), preserved in duck fat

12 chicken wings

3 shallots, peeled and thinly sliced

2 leeks, cleaned and thinly sliced

3 quarts duck stock, or good flavorsome chicken stock

6 slices fresh foie gras

sea salt and freshly ground black pepper

Place the beans in a pan with the garlic. Cover with clean water, bring to a boil, skim, reduce to a simmer, and cook for approximately 2½ hours so the beans are thoroughly cooked but not falling apart. Once cooked, remove from the heat but keep in their water.

Bring your preserved giblets out of the fridge so that the fat warms up, making it easy to scrape it off. Take a pot large enough for all your ingredients, drop in a spot of duck fat, place it on the heat, and when hot, brown the chicken wings. When these are a satisfactory color, remove from the pot and keep to one side. Now, in the same fat, sweat the shallots and leeks until soft but not burnt, return the chicken wings to the pot, add the stock and drained beans, bring to a boil, skim, and reduce to a simmer. When the chicken wings are thoroughly cooked but not falling apart, add the necks, hearts, and gizzards. When these are heated through the dish is ready; it should be loose and brothy, not thick and stewy. Season with salt and pepper.

Just before serving, float the slices of foie gras on top of the stew, the heat from which will start to melt it. Serve in deep bowls and eat with plenty of crusty white bread.

POACHED SALTED DUCK LEGS

This is a dish you have to think about a week ahead.

6 duck legs, which you have
   kept in a brine (see
   page 76) for a week, rinsed

1 head of garlic, skin on

2 whole carrots, peeled

2 leeks, cleaned

2 stalks of celery

2 onions, peeled and halved

2 bay leaves

a bundle of fresh herbs tied
   together

12 black peppercorns

Place the duck legs in a pot with all the other
ingredients. Cover with clean water, bring gently to a
boil, then reduce to a calm simmer and cook for
approximately 1 hour: you want them giving but not
completely falling from the bone. Serve with lentils, as
with boiled pork belly (page 74).

DUCK LEGS AND CARROTS

duck fat or unsalted butter

6 duck legs (available without the rest of the duck from most butchers)

1 onion, peeled and sliced

2 leeks, cleaned and sliced

8 cloves of garlic, peeled and kept whole

14 medium-sized carrots, peeled and chopped into ¼-inch rounds

a bundle of parsley and 4 sprigs of rosemary (you have to be very careful with rosemary, since delicious as it is, it can take over) tied together

2 bay leaves

1 chile, kept whole

sea salt and freshly ground black pepper

about 1¾ cups chicken stock

Get a frying pan hot, add a spoonful of duck fat or butter, wait until it is sizzling, and then brown the duck legs on both sides. Remove from the pan and set aside. In the same pan cook the onion, leeks, and garlic. Mix in the carrots and cook for 3 more minutes, then decant all the vegetables into a deep ovenproof dish.

Nestle in the herb bundle, bay leaves, and chile (this just emits a slight warmth to the dish, unlike a more pungent chopped chile). Press the duck legs into the carrot bed, skin side upward, season the dish with salt and pepper, and pour chicken stock over until the duck legs are showing like alligators in a swamp. Place in a medium to hot 375°F oven for 1½ hours, keeping an eye on it so it does not burn—if it threatens to, cover the dish with foil. Check the legs with a knife; you want them thoroughly giving.

When cooked the carrots will have drawn up the duck fat and the stock reduced to a rich juice; the duck skin should be brown and crispy. Serve with bread to mop up the juices and follow with a green salad.

SALTED DUCK LEGS, GREEN BEANS, AND CORNMEAL DUMPLINGS

The dumplings are made with a recipe of Stephanie Alexander's and are so splendid I cannot improve on them in any way. I hope she does not mind my using it, as they are ideal companions to the salted duck legs.

6 duck legs, brined (see page 76) for a week, rinsed

1 head of garlic, skin on

2 whole carrots, peeled

2 leeks, cleaned

2 stalks of celery

2 onions, peeled and halved

2 bay leaves

a bundle of fresh herbs tied

12 black peppercorns

DUMPLINGS

2 eggs

7 ounces (about 5 firmly packed cups) finely diced whole wheat bread

2 tablespoons duck fat

2 ounces minced smoked bacon

⅔ cup finely grated fresh horseradish

¾ cup fine yellow cornmeal

sea salt and freshly ground black pepper

FINISHING

2 pounds haricots verts, topped and tailed

Cook your duck legs as in Poached Salted Duck Legs (page 110), and while they're simmering combine all the dumpling ingredients together into a sticky mixture; it should not be dry. Roll into ¾-inch balls; you should have 12 dumplings.

Fifteen minutes before the duck legs are ready, ladle out some of the cooking liquor into another pan. Bring it to a gentle simmer and cook your dumplings in this for about 10 minutes. When the duck legs are ready, remove from the liquor and keep warm and moist. Strain the liquor, then return it to the pot. Bring to a rolling boil and cook the beans for 3 to 4 minutes.

Serve in a deep plate or shallow bowl, with the beans at the bottom, and the duck legs and dumplings on top. Pour over a ladle of cooking liquor and eat.

BOILED CHICKEN, LEEKS, AND AÏOLI

This may sound complicated, but it's actually quite simple and is emphatically worth it.

1 free-range chicken (slit the skin between the leg and breast)

2 carrots, peeled

10 leeks, trimmed and cleaned

1 onion, peeled

1 whole head of garlic, skin on

2 stalks of celery, chopped

2 bay leaves

a bundle of thyme, parsley, and rosemary tied together

black peppercorns

sea salt

Aïoli (page 162)

Place the bird and all the ingredients except 8 of the leeks and the aïoli in a large pot, cover with cold water, and bring to a boil. As soon as the pot boils cover it with a lid, take it off the heat, and leave it to cool.

Remove the cooled chicken from the stock. Strain the stock, then return it with the chicken to a clean pot, retaining enough of the stock for another pot for your 8 leeks. Bring the stock up to a gentle simmer. Now immerse your chicken for 30 minutes to heat through thoroughly; you will now have a moist bird without its falling apart or being toughened from hard boiling. Bring the stock for the leeks to a boil, drop them in, and cook them for 8 to 10 minutes, depending on their size.

Serve the chicken and leeks with a splash of the chicken stock, a bowl of the aïoli, and coarse sea salt. As with any boiled unbrined meat, coarse sea salt applied just before eating is very good. Save the rest of the stock for future cooking.

CHICKEN AND PIG'S TROTTER

3 pig's trotters (see page 38)

2 carrots, peeled

1 whole head of garlic, skin on

2 onions, peeled and halved

a bundle of fresh herbs tied together

2 bay leaves

2 stalks of celery, chopped

1 leek, cleaned

12 black peppercorns

1 bottle of red wine

2 quarts chicken stock

duck fat or unsalted butter

1 pound smoked streaky bacon (see page 79), rind removed in one piece, rolled and tied, and bacon cut into chunks

12 shallots, peeled

1 chicken, cut into serving pieces and seasoned with salt and freshly ground black pepper

In a pan place the trotters, carrots, garlic, onions, herb bundle, bay leaves, celery, leek, and peppercorns, cover with wine and chicken stock, cover with the lid, and place in a medium 350°F oven for 3 hours until the trotters are thoroughly cooked. Remove the trotters from the pan and allow to cool until handleable. Strain the remaining liquor into a clean pan, discard the vegetables, and place on the heat. Bring to a simmer and allow to reduce. Meanwhile your trotters have cooled, so pluck the skin and flesh off the bones and add this to your simmering sauce, and cook for 1 hour. Then get a frying pan hot, add duck fat or butter and brown the bacon rind and shallots, and add these to your simmering pot (do not clean the frying pan); let this all cook together for a further 30 minutes.

Meanwhile, in the frying pan you have kept, brown your pieces of chicken. Place the chicken in an ovenproof dish, then pour over it the trotter skin and meat, chunks of bacon, shallot-rind mixture, and the juice. Check for seasoning, as the bacon will give saltiness. Cover and place in a hot 425°F oven for 40 minutes, then uncover for 10 minutes more. When it's ready, serve straightaway with mashed potatoes. A delicious extra for dipping in the sauce is triangles of white bread fried in duck fat.

PHEASANT AND PIG'S TROTTER PIE WITH SUET CRUST

A PIE FOR SIX

This is a most rich and steadying pie.

FILLING

3 pig's trotters (see page 38)

a bundle of fresh herbs

1 head of garlic, skin on

2 bay leaves

10 black peppercorns

2 stalks of celery, chopped

2 red onions, peeled and halved

2 carrots, peeled

1 bottle of red wine

1¾ quarts chicken stock

a scoop of duck fat or unsalted butter

1 pound unsmoked streaky bacon (see page 79), rind removed, rolled, and tied, bacon cut into chunks

2 pheasants, split in half, kept on the bone, and seasoned with salt and freshly ground black pepper

3 onions, peeled and sliced

The pie filling is best made the day before, to find itself. Place the trotters in a pot with the herbs, garlic, bay leaves, peppercorns, celery, red onions, and carrots, cover with red wine and stock, bring to a boil, then reduce to a simmer and cook for 3 hours, until the trotters are cooked and tender. Remove the trotters from the pot, then strain the stock. While the trotters are warm pick the flesh and skin from the bones.

Get a frying pan hot, add duck fat or butter, fry the bacon chunks and the rolled rind, then remove to a deep roasting pan or ovenproof dish. Now brown the pheasant halves, and then move them to join the bacon (if the pan is looking dry add a little more fat). Then sweat the onions, add these to the roasting pan, add the trotter flesh and stock, and cover with aluminum foil. Place in a hot 425°F oven for 15 minutes, then reduce the heat to 350°F and cook for another 30 minutes. Remove, check the seasoning, and allow to cool in the stock (at this point it can be eaten if you have not the patience for making a pie).

When cool remove the pheasant and pull the meat off the bones, keeping the pieces of flesh large, as you want them to maintain their integrity in the pie. Return them to the other ingredients and refrigerate overnight.

BIRDS AND GAME

115

1½ cups self-rising flour

¼ pound suet, shredded
(fresh if possible, ask your
butcher)

a healthy pinch of sea salt

1 egg yolk, beaten, for glaze

To make the pastry, mix the ingredients (except the egg yolk) together, then add ice-cold water cautiously, to achieve a firm dough. Allow this to rest in the fridge for at least 2 hours before use.

Place your meat mixture in a pie dish (if there appears to be too much sauce, hold some back, it will come in handy somewhere else), cover with pastry, paint this with egg yolk, and bake in a medium to hot 375°F oven for 40 minutes. When the pastry is ready and golden, and the stuffing bubbling inside, serve and eat. Very good with Brussels sprouts.

RABBITS AND HARES There are two types of rabbits to choose from, the wild or the tame. The pros and cons are as follows: with wild you need a good source, as they are often badly shot up or mauled by ferrets, which tends to leave them as an off-putting mess of blood clots. What you need is a good shot, who can get them cleanly in the head. Wild rabbits can vary in flavor and texture according to where they come from. Some seem to have had an easier time of it compared to others, whose lives have been full of angst. These differences are apparent in the eating, their lifestyles being reflected in their flesh. This is a regional phenomenon, so as well as finding a good shot, it is good to know where your rabbit harks from.

Though prone to slightly tougher flesh wild rabbits have more flavor than tame rabbits, which make for more subtle eating and are much larger and meatier, more consistent, and of course do not suffer from the same wounds as the wild. A tame rabbit will certainly feed four. A wild rabbit will feed between two and three, depending on its size. Each has its appropriateness for differing dishes.

A hare is almost another creature altogether. A much more dark and gamey beast, it requires a completely different approach to cooking, as will come clear in the following recipes.

SADDLE OF RABBIT

From a good butcher you should be able to obtain just the saddles of rabbit; if not, you can always use the legs for something else (try confit, page 98). You will need a tame rabbit or a particularly happy wild rabbit for this dish. Take the fillets off the bone (2 per portion if tame, 3 if wild) with a thin, sharp knife, following the backbone and ribs, or ask your butcher. Remove the kidneys and save them.

4 tame or 6 wild rabbit saddles, with the rabbit kidneys, cut off the bone into 8 or 12 fillets

sea salt and freshly ground black pepper

1 pound thinly sliced unsmoked streaky bacon (see page 79) or fatback

a bundle of of caul fat (your butcher should have no problem obtaining this for you)

olive oil

Roughly chop the kidneys. Lay out 4 fillets, on which you apply the chopped kidneys. Season with salt and pepper then sandwich with the remaining fillets. Roll these in streaky bacon and then in a thin layer of caul fat to hold them together, to produce a kind of rabbit and bacon cigar.

Get an ovenproof frying pan hot, apply a spot of oil, and let this heat up. Then brown your rabbit rolls thoroughly (this is very important, as you want to crisp up and cook away the caul fat, so you do not end up with a stringy, chewy, fatty outside). When the rolls are a pleasing brown, place the frying pan in a hot 400 to 425°F oven for 10 to 12 minutes. You want to catch the flesh just as it loses its pink translucent quality.

Serve the rolls with a salad that captures the spirit of the garden, made up from, for example, scallions, baby carrots, radishes, peas, fava beans (if in season), rocket (arugula), and chopped parsley (and a subliminal caper if you feel so inclined—I do!). Dress with Vinaigrette (page 161) and eat with the succulent rabbit.

RABBIT AND GARLIC

There was a wonderful rabbit I ate in Barcelona, which was dry but wet, salty but not too salty, and above all garlicky. This recipe came out of attempting to recreate it. In fact, except for the garlic it is nothing like it, but still delicious nonetheless.

2 healthy splashes of olive oil

2 tame rabbits, chopped into sections (if you don't have a cleaver or a heavy knife, ask your butcher to do this)

sea salt and freshly ground black pepper

⅔ pound smoked streaky bacon (see page 79), cut into spirited chunks, rind removed in one piece and reserved

24 shallots, peeled and kept whole

60 to 80 cloves of garlic, skin on

1⅓ cups dry sherry

2½ cups white wine

1 quart chicken stock

2 bay leaves

a bundle of fresh thyme and parsley tied together

Get a large ovenproof pot with a lid, place on the heat, and pour in enough olive oil to just cover the bottom. Season the rabbit pieces with salt and pepper and when the oil is hot brown the rabbit. When you are happy with the hue, remove them from the pot (if all the oil has gone with them add another splash). Put in the bacon, its rind, and the shallots, allow to sizzle, and stir for 10 minutes, not letting them burn. Now return the rabbit to the pot and add the garlic, sherry, wine, stock, bay leaves, and finally the bundle of thyme and parsley. Check the seasoning. Bring to a boil, straightaway reduce to a simmer, place the lid on, and put the pot into a warm to hot 350°F to 375°F oven for approximately 1½ hours, but keep an eye on it and check the meat for giving qualities with a sharp knife (not quite but soon to fall off the bone).

Serve hot straight from the pot, encouraging your fellow diners to suck the flesh from the unpeeled garlic cloves, which will now be sweet and delicious. For the juices you will need both bread and napkins.

RABBIT WRAPPED IN FENNEL AND BACON

A tame rabbit will certainly feed four. A wild rabbit will feed between two or three, depending on its size.

1 whole wild or tame rabbit

a healthy splash of extra-virgin olive oil

sea salt and freshly ground black pepper

a bundle of the stems of dried fennel (which can be obtained from good food shops, or you can pick and dry them yourself)

20 slices smoked streaky bacon (see page 79)

4 heads of garlic, skin on

¼ bottle of white wine

2 cups chicken stock

Splash and rub your rabbit with oil, season enthusiastically with salt and pepper, then surround with the dried fennel from end to end and tummy to back (so it starts to look like a scene from *The Wicker Man*). Hold these in place by wrapping the whole thing in the strips of streaky bacon.

Lay in a deepish roasting pan or dish, nestle the garlic next to the rabbit, pour the wine and stock around it, and roast in a medium to hot 375°F oven for approximately 1½ hours, depending on the size of the rabbit (tame ones may only take 1 hour); check with a knife in its thigh to see if it is giving. The aim of this dish is a rabbit that's well cooked, but still moist thanks to the insulation we have provided.

When cooked remove the fennel. Unfortunately it is not edible, but the bacon should be wonderfully crispy. With a cleaver or heavy knife, chop the rabbit into chunks and serve with the garlic and a jug of the juices from the pan.

RABBIT WITH PEA AND FAVA BEAN PURÉE

This dish lends itself to the gentler flesh of tame rabbit, rather than wild. You could substitute chicken.

a splash of olive oil

1 tame rabbit, cut up and seasoned with salt and freshly ground black pepper

2 leeks, cleaned and chopped

1 good-sized potato, peeled and chopped

1 onion, peeled and chopped

2 quarts chicken stock

2 cloves of garlic, peeled and chopped

a bundle of thyme and parsley tied together

2 to 2¼ pounds fresh peas in the pod, shelled

2 to 2¼ pounds fresh fava beans in the pod, shelled and peeled

a handful of fresh mint, leaves only, chopped just before using

Vinaigrette (page 161)

Take a pot large enough to fit all the ingredients, add a splash of olive oil, and get it hot. Lightly brown your pieces of rabbit, then remove; add the leeks, potato, and onion. Sweat these—not too much coloring—and return the rabbit to the pan. Cover it with stock and add the garlic and herbs. Check the seasoning and bring it gently to a boil, then reduce to a very gentle simmer and cook for 40 minutes. Remove the rabbit, moisten it with a splash of stock, and keep it warm. Bring the stock and vegetables back to a boil, add the peas and beans, and boil for 5 minutes, until they are cooked but not mushy and losing their color. Now strain the contents of your pot, keeping the stock (this will make wonderful soup) and the vegetables separate. Place the vegetables in the food processor and puree (if they are too dry add some of the stock).

Check the seasoning and mix the mint with the vinaigrette.

Serve the purée with the rabbit, over which you pour some of the minty vinaigrette, and accompany it with hot beets. The combination of colors looks very fine and it tastes fantastic.

JELLIED RABBIT

Use tame or particularly beautiful wild rabbits for this. Be warned, this takes about 2 days to prepare.

1 tame rabbit or 2 wild rabbits, chopped up but bone in (if tame, you may get 3 sections out of the saddle)

10 shallots, peeled and finely sliced

1 bottle of white wine

2 pig's trotters (see page 38)

2 heads of garlic, skin on

a bundle of thyme tied together

10 black peppercorns

1 quart light chicken stock

¾ to 1 pound thinly sliced unsmoked streaky bacon (see page 79)

2 bay leaves

sea salt and freshly ground black pepper

Marinate the rabbit and shallots in the white wine in a nonmetal container in the fridge overnight. Meanwhile, place the trotters in a pot with the garlic, thyme, and peppercorns, cover with the chicken stock, and bring them to a gentle simmer. Cover, and keeping an eye on it cook for 3 hours. Strain (if you want to you can add the trotter flesh to the final dish, otherwise discard it), return the liquid to a pan, and reduce by half. Allow to cool.

Next day, line an ovenproof covered crock with the bacon. Mix the rabbit and shallot-wine marinade with the trotter stock (this may have jelled so it might have to be melted) and bay leaves. Check the seasoning, remembering the salty bacon factor, and also that you will be eating it cold so it will need a flavor boost. Pour the rabbit and its mixture into the lined crock, cover, and place in a medium 350°F oven for 2½ hours, keeping an eye on it so it never cooks too fast. Check with a small, sharp knife that the rabbit is cooked. When cooked allow the whole crock to cool and then place it in the fridge overnight. Next day, serve cold from the crock with hot boiled potatoes with lots of chopped curly parsley.

CONFIT OF RABBIT LEG IN BROTH

This is an excellent way of using your rabbit legs after making the boned Saddle of Rabbit on page 117. They will need to be turned into confit first, though.

4 rabbit hind legs

12 shallots, peeled and kept whole

12 small turnips (if possible with greens, cut off but kept)

12 baby carrots, greens cut off and discarded

sea salt and freshly ground black pepper

Aïoli (page 162)

Make a stock with the rabbit bones (see page 3). If there are not enough, add chicken bones.

Confit your rabbit using the method on page 98. If you have some ready, so much the better. Get it out of the fridge so that it comes to kitchen temperature and it's easy to wipe most of the fat off with your fingers.

Bring your stock to a boil and add the shallots. Cook for 10 minutes, then add the rest of the vegetables, except the turnip greens. Cook for another 8 minutes, then reduce the broth to a gentle simmer. Add the rabbit legs and let them gently heat through and soften. When they are ready and the vegetables are cooked, add the turnip greens and allow them to wilt; season to taste with salt and pepper. Serve in deep plates or shallow bowls so a ladle of broth can be poured over each serving. Eat with aïoli.

JUGGED HARE

The hare's blood is vital for this dish, so if you are not gutting the beast yourself, ask your butcher to make sure they reserve any blood. It is important to mix a small splash of red wine vinegar into the blood as soon as possible to prevent its curdling, something I am sure the butcher will do for you if you are not there at the moment of gutting and chopping.

3½ cups all-purpose flour

1 teaspoon ground mace

1 teaspoon ground cloves

1 teaspoon ground allspice

sea salt and freshly ground black pepper

1 hare, gutted and cut up, blood reserved and mixed with a small splash of red wine vinegar

1 generous teaspoon unsalted butter

3 red onions, peeled and chopped

3 carrots, peeled and chopped

3 stalks of celery, chopped

2 leeks, cleaned and chopped

½ bottle of red wine

a mixed bundle of fresh herbs tied together

2 cloves of garlic, peeled

2 bay leaves

2 quarts chicken stock

1 cup port

Mix together the flour, mace, cloves, allspice, and salt and pepper, and roll your pieces of hare in this. At the same time heat the butter in a large pan. Brown the floured hare gently in the pan (it is important to do this just as the hare has been floured, as otherwise the flour coating will go damp and sticky and *globdulate*). When brown, remove the hare and add the vegetables to the pan. Cook to achieve a nice color, but not burnt. Return the hare to the pan with the wine, herbs, garlic, and bay leaves, season cautiously, cover with chicken stock, cover, and place in a low to medium 325°F oven for 3 hours.

When cooked, remove the hare from the mixture and strain the liquor. Discard the vegetables. You can prepare the dish ahead up to this point. Return the hare to the liquor, allow it to cool, and set it aside, preferably in the fridge unless you are eating it the same day. To make a sauce, remove the hare and return the liquor to the heat, add the port, and boil quickly for 5 minutes. Reduce the heat so the sauce is not boiling (very important), stir in the blood, and allow the sauce to thicken. Return the hare to the sauce and serve with mashed potatoes.

ANOTHER THEORY OF JUGGED HARE (AND POSSIBILITIES FOR HARE FILLETS)

YOU WILL NEED 2 HARES TO FEED FOUR

This entails two days of eating hare. On the first day you have the saddle, and you jug the legs, but keep the legs for the next day.

The first day

Remove the back and front legs and shoulders, but keep the saddles whole. My feeling is that the legs lend themselves perfectly to jugging, but the leaner saddles have a habit of drying out. So to do them justice, fillet the saddles (just follow the bones with a sharp knife), season, get an ovenproof frying pan very hot, add butter, and allow it to sizzle. Sear the fillets in the pan and place in a hot 450°F oven for 4 minutes. Remove the fillets to a warm plate, put them in a warm place, and allow them to rest for 10 minutes. Serve with delicious, rich mashed parsnips. This is wonderful.

The second day

Reheat the legs gently in a pan with the lid on in a medium 350°F oven and follow with the port and blood procedure described in Jugged Hare, page 123. Do not allow the blood to boil. This may seem like a lot of hare for one weekend, but I feel it does more justice to the various bits of the animal.

BRAISED FRONT LEG AND SHOULDER OF VENISON

TO FEED APPROXIMATELY EIGHT

Before you embark on this, make sure you have a roasting pan large enough for one leg and whole shoulder of venison. You can, if you need to, cut the leg at the joint, to make it fit.

duck fat or unsalted butter

1 pound unsmoked streaky bacon (see page 79), rind removed in one piece, cut into chunks

6 carrots, peeled and chopped

6 leeks, cleaned and chopped

4 onions, peeled and sliced

¾ to 1 pound fresh cèpes (porcini)—imagine the deer running through the woods, trampling wild mushrooms—or 1 to 2 ounces dried, soaked in 2½ cups hot water for 2 hours

1 front leg and shoulder of venison

12 cloves of garlic, peeled

a bundle of fresh herbs tied together

sea salt and freshly ground black pepper

1 bottle of red wine

1 quart chicken stock

Place your roasting pan on the stove, melt the duck fat or butter, and sweat the bacon, bacon rind, and vegetables until they soften. Add the drained cèpes (reserving the mushroom water), cook for another 4 minutes, then nestle in the venison, garlic, and herbs. Season with salt and pepper, add the wine, stock, and strained mushroom water, cover with aluminum foil, and place in a medium 350°F oven for 3 to 3½ hours. Because of the cartilage and fat at this end of the animal, the meat should not dry out as venison is prone to do, but remain tender and even *unctuous*. Serve with its accompanying vegetables and juices, and mashed potatoes.

FISH
AND
SHELLFISH

CRAB AND MAYONNAISE

This probably does not count as a recipe, more like a few thoughts. Preferably you want to get your crabs alive. Some say you should kill them before placing them into boiling water, as this is kinder to the crab: turn them over, and there is a flap; lift this to reveal a slight dip, then with something like a knitting needle and hammer, spear the crab, aiming toward the front of the crab and down. I am afraid I just drop the living crab into boiling water, which must be as salty as the sea; otherwise, water will leach into the crab, resulting in wet flesh. Cooking time depends on the crab's size; as a rough guide, for the first pound allow 15 minutes, then another 5 minutes per further pound.

When it's cold remove the main shell, and clean out the "dead men's fingers," which are grayish, coarse, slightly fluffy gills on each side of the central body. Once this is done everything else is edible. Eat and enjoy with suitable tools to assist you in cracking open the claws and scraping out the meat from tight corners. There is almost nothing finer than a lunch spent wrestling with a crab. Keep the shells for stock.

Eat with Mayonnaise (page 163) that is not too stiff. If stiff, this does not make a friendly partner for your crab.

DEVILED CRAB

This recipe is from Su Rogers, my best friend's mum—I beg her pardon for altering it a little, for I recall more of the meat is picked out of the shell in her recipe, whereas I enjoy the hard work at the eating moment. It is also the only dish in this cookbook which contains cilantro.

3 crabs, 2 to 2¼ pounds each

a healthy splash of olive oil

4 cloves of garlic, peeled and very finely chopped

2 fresh red chiles, seeds removed, very finely chopped

¼ pound fresh ginger, peeled and very finely grated

12 spring onions or scallions, cleaned, trimmed, and chopped

juice of 2 lemons

sea salt and freshly ground black pepper

half a bunch of washed cilantro, leaves only, just disciplined by the merest chopping

half a bunch of flat-leaf parsley, leaves only, just disciplined by the merest chopping

Cook and prepare the crabs as on page 129. For this recipe you want to boil them for 20 minutes, on the side of undercooked rather than overcooked, as they are cooked again. Scoop all the meat out of the shell into a bowl and remove all the legs from the bodies. With a strong knife, cut the bodies into quarters and partially crack the large claws with a hammer.

In a pan heat the olive oil and fry the garlic, chile, and ginger for 3 minutes. Add the quartered crab bodies, the claws, the spring onions, and then the scooped crabmeat and all the legs, and the lemon juice. Season with salt and pepper and stir continuously and enthusiastically until heated through.

Just before serving, throw in the cilantro and parsley, give one last stir, tip into a dish, and eat armed with useful tools to pick out the crab flesh, and many napkins, and, for that matter, much white wine.

KEDGEREE

Kedgeree harks back to the days of the British Raj, starting as a dish of rice and lentils way back. But as with many dishes, much alteration has taken place over time. And now here is my very basic kedgeree, ideal for eating morning, noon, or night. It is very good by itself, but does go very well with Green Bean Chutney (page 172).

Natural smoked haddock is exactly what it says it is—smoked haddock. There are the yellow fillets of cured haddock, which have been dyed to give the impression of being smoked. The natural is obviously preferable.

2 sides of natural smoked haddock

much unsalted butter

2 cups long-grain rice

sea salt

2 red onions, peeled and sliced

1 lemon

freshly ground black pepper

4 hard-boiled free-range eggs, peeled and roughly chopped

a big handful of chopped curly parsley

Place the haddock fillets in a roasting pan with healthy knobs of butter and 1 cup of water and cook in a hot 425°F oven for 10 minutes. Remove them from the oven, allow them to cool, skin and roughly flake them. Save the juice in the pan. Place the rice in another pan, lay your hand flat on the rice, and add water until your hand is covered. Add a pinch of salt, bring to a boil, cover, and simmer for about 20 minutes, then check the rice and drain off any excess water.

Gently fry the onions in butter in a big frying pan, so that they go soft and sweet rather than brown and burnt. Add the fish and rice and the liquor from the haddock pan, adding more butter if the mixture seems dry or is sticking (this dish is a very good vehicle for butter). When all the ingredients are heated through, squeeze the lemon over, season with salt and pepper, stir in the eggs and parsley, season again, and serve.

SMOKED HADDOCK, MUSTARD, AND SAFFRON

A version of a medieval dish, very yellow and delicious.

1 cup white wine

½ cup water

a splash of white wine vinegar

½ teaspoon Coleman's Dry English Mustard Powder

a healthy pinch of saffron

freshly ground black pepper

2 medium fillets of natural smoked haddock, evenly cut in half

a largish knob of unsalted butter

Mix together the wine, water, vinegar, mustard powder, saffron, and pepper. Place your pieces of smoked haddock in an ovenproof frying pan, pour the wine and saffron mixture over them, loosely cover with aluminum foil, and place in a medium to hot 375°F oven for approximately 15 minutes, until all is piping hot. Remove from the oven, place the fish on a warm, deep plate, put the pan of sauce on the heat, and allow to boil. Add the butter and stir briskly until the sauce and butter have emulsified. Now pour over the fish and serve hot with mashed potatoes.

SOFT ROES ON TOAST

Perfect for breakfast, light lunch, high tea, or as a savory with a glass of port. A rich buttery treat.

Soft roes are in fact herring semen. When filleting a herring for pickling save the soft roes, which are the white creamy sacs, not the granular orange sacs. Otherwise, your fishmonger is bound to have some. Enquire about fresh, although it does freeze very well as long as it is treated properly once defrosted; it needs to be handled gently, otherwise it can end up as a creamy mess.

1¾ sticks (14 tablespoons) unsalted butter

4 pieces of white toast

1 pound soft roes, still reasonably intact in their sacs

sea salt and freshly ground black pepper

juice of 1 lemon

chopped curly parsley, optional (some feel the dish needs this element of green; I do not)

Get a frying pan hot, melt the butter until bubbling, have the toast ready, and place the roes in the pan. They will curl up. Cook for 3 to 4 minutes each side, allowing the roes to brown slightly. Season with salt and pepper, and just before placing on the toast, add the lemon juice (and the chopped parsley if you wish) to the now foaming butter.

Place the roes on the toast, pour the butter over them, and eat.

FISH PIE

Even just writing this recipe down, its soothing qualities have quite restored me from the fragile state in which I was.

3 fillets of natural smoked haddock

10 black peppercorns

3⅓ cups milk

3¼ to 3½ pounds potatoes, peeled and cut into quarters

2 sticks plus 1 tablespoon unsalted butter, and more still

¾ cup all-purpose flour

four 10-minute hard-boiled free-range eggs, peeled and minimally chopped

sea salt and freshly ground black pepper

In an ovenproof dish, cover the smoked haddock and peppercorns with 2 cups of the milk and bake in a medium to hot 375°F oven for approximately 20 minutes. Check whether the fish has cooked through: it should easily flake when prodded with a knife. Remove it from the milk, strain and save the milk, and flake the flesh off the haddock skins into hearty bite-size chunks.

Meanwhile, boil your potatoes. When they are cooked, drain and mash them, blend in the rest of the milk and 10 tablespoons of the butter, and season with salt and pepper. While the potatoes are boiling, melt the remaining 7 tablespoons of butter in a non-aluminum pan, and when it's starting to bubble, add the flour and stir until the mixture smells biscuity (this suggests the flour is cooked), but do not let the mixture change color. There must be no browning at all, so be cautious with the heat. Then add the warm fish milk, whisking as you go to avoid lumps (whisking in aluminum would turn the sauce a nasty gray). Let the sauce thicken until it easily coats the back of your spoon, and check the seasoning.

Now we are ready to construct the fish pie. In a pie dish place your haddock and hard-boiled eggs. Pour your fishy white sauce over, leaving room for you to spread on the top layer of potatoes. Then run a fork across the top of the potatoes, as if plowing a field. This is not for mere decoration, but aids the crisping-up factor.

Dot the top with little knobs of butter, place the pie in a hot 425°F oven, and cook for 30 minutes or until piping hot and golden brown. Serve with boiled peas.

MUSSELS GRILLED ON A BARBECUE

Ideally you are on a Hebridean island, eating mussels you have picked and cooked on driftwood. If this cannot be, the barbecue in the backyard will suffice very well. P.S. This works just as well for large clams or razor clams.

8 pounds mussels, cleaned

2 healthy handfuls of curly parsley, finely chopped

2 healthy handfuls of celery leaves, lightly chopped

DRESSING

juice of 2 lemons

4 cloves of garlic, crushed

1 tablespoon young soft thyme leaves, chopped

1⅔ cups extra-virgin olive oil

sea salt and freshly ground black pepper

Get your barbecue to that perfect glowing moment (preferably using wood with a good history, as I am sure this helps the flavor) and simply throw your mussels on the grill. The joy of this is they now simply cook in their own juices.

As soon as they open, scoop them up into an appropriate bowl, add the parsley, celery leaves, and dressing, and toss thoroughly. Eat while hot.

SALTING COD AND LINGCOD

1 cod or lingcod, beheaded, cleaned, and slit open the length of the underside

plenty of coarse sea salt

Open the fish up flat (this will entail some careful cutting through bones), then with a handful of salt and a kitchen towel gently remove any remaining blood.

In a glass or plastic dish sprinkle a layer of salt, lay your fish on this, then cover it with salt and place it in the fridge. Check it each day and tip off any liquid and add dry salt as necessary. Once the fish is firm and has ceased to emit liquid (approximately 10 days), remove from its dish, leaving the salt that has adhered to the fish attached, tie string around its tail, and hang in a dry airy place. It does not have to be cold, but must not be hot. Leave until it is dry and firm. This process should take approximately three weeks, but keep prodding and squeezing to test its firmness.

When you want to use it, cut off the amount you are going to cook with and soak in running water (or certainly regularly change the water) for at least 12 hours.

Once soaked the salt fish should be refrigerated.

SALT COD, POTATO, AND TOMATO

TO SERVE SIX

1¾ pounds tomatoes (vine or plum are probably most appropriate), cut in half lengthwise, the green hard piece where the stem meets the tomato removed

24 cloves of garlic, peeled

sea salt and freshly ground black pepper

1 cup extra-virgin olive oil

3¼ to 3½ pounds flavorsome potatoes, peeled and cut into chunks, pebbles-on-the-beach style—everything does not have to be cut in the same dimension. There can be an element of randomness, just as there is with pebbles on the beach.

2 to 2¼ pounds salt cod of the lightly salted variety (see page 137), soaked overnight, then skinned and cut into 1¼-inch chunks

a big handful of curly parsley, chopped

3 hard-boiled free-range eggs, peeled and chopped

Place your tomatoes and garlic in an ovenproof dish, and sprinkle with salt and pepper and a healthy coating of extra-virgin olive oil. Cook in a medium 350°F oven until cooked soft and giving (check whether the garlic is cooked as well; if not remove the tomatoes to a bowl, leaving the garlic in the tomatoey oil, and return it to the oven until cooked). Hang on to the tomatoey oil.

Meanwhile, cook your potatoes in gently boiling salted water. Also bring another pan of clean water to a gentle bubbling simmer, which you will cook the cod in.

When the potatoes, tomatoes, and garlic are ready, poach the salt cod gently for 5 minutes. Then in a bowl bring together the drained potatoes and cod, the tomatoes and garlic with their oil, and the parsley, and season and mix gently (the cod will crumble, which is fine). Top with the eggs and serve.

SALT COD AND BEANS

TO SERVE SIX

Fish sticks and baked beans grow up.

1 pound dried white haricot
   beans, soaked overnight

1 head of garlic, skin on, plus
   12 cloves, peeled and
   quartered

2 bay leaves

2 onions, peeled and sliced

2 heads of fennel, sliced
   across the grain

olive oil

1¾ pounds fresh chorizo,
   a variety suitable for
   cooking, sliced into ½-
   inch-thick rounds

5 canned plum tomatoes

a bundle of fresh herbs tied
   together

1 quart chicken stock

sea salt and freshly ground
   black pepper

2 to 2¼ pounds salt cod of
   the lightly salted variety
   (see page 137), soaked
   overnight, cut into 6 pieces

Drain the beans from their soaking water, cover in clean cold water in a pan, add the head of garlic and the bay leaves, bring to a boil, reduce to a simmer, and cook for approximately 2 hours. When thoroughly cooked, remove from the heat and drain, keeping the bean juice.

Meanwhile, in another pan sweat the onions, garlic cloves, and fennel in olive oil until soft, then add the chorizo, followed very shortly by the tomatoes, crushed in your hands as you place them in the pan. Nestle in the bundle of herbs and let this mixture cook for another 20 minutes, then add the beans and enough stock to just cover all the ingredients (if you do not have enough stock, use bean water). Simmer for 1 hour, allowing all the ingredients to acclimatize to each other.

Bring a pan of clean water to a gentle simmer, and when your beans are ready and you have checked them for seasoning, poach the salt cod pieces for 6 to 8 minutes in the water. Finally, carefully lift and drain the cod, and serve on top of a mound of your beans.

HAIRY TATTIES

In a fish market on the east coast of Scotland we came across salt ling (a poor relation of cod). Intrigued, we were also given this recipe. The name refers to the fact that the fibrous nature of the salt fish, when mashed with the potatoes, gives them a hairy appearance. The salty fishy potato goes incredibly well with boiled egg; there seems to be a natural affinity between these elements. This is a splendid dish. If you can't find salt ling, use salt cod, which is a fine substitute.

3¼ to 3½ pounds salt ling (see page 137), soaked in frequent changes of cold water for 12 hours

2 whole onions, peeled

3 bay leaves

4¼ to 4½ pounds floury potatoes, such as Idaho russets, peeled

1 cup milk

2 sticks unsalted butter

freshly ground black pepper and possibly sea salt

6 free-range eggs

Put the ling in a pan of fresh water with the onions and bay leaves, bring to a boil, then turn down to a simmer for 14 minutes.

Meanwhile, place your potatoes in unsalted water, bring to a boil, and cook until soft enough to mash. Then hardboil your eggs so that the yolks are soft and slightly giving (about 8 minutes).

Drain the fish, discarding the onions and bay leaves, let it cool until you can handle it, then pull the flesh away from the skin and bones—be warned, this is a very sticky exercise.

You should now have warm salt fish and drained hot potatoes. Heat the milk and butter, add half to the potatoes, and mash. Add the fish flesh, and keep mashing; you should start to have a pan of hairy mashed potatoes. If they are too stiff add a little more milk and butter. Check for seasoning—it will certainly need black pepper but depending on the fish you may or may not need salt.

Serve a hairy mound with a hard-boiled egg in its shell.

SALT COD, POTATO, AND GARLIC PURÉE

This puree is the St. John version of brandade de morue.

1¼ to 1½ pounds salt cod (see page 137), soaked for over 12 hours in cold water (changed as often as possible)

⅔ pound floury potatoes, such as Idaho russets, peeled and cut into quarters

sea salt

2 cups milk

2 cups extra-virgin olive oil

12 garlic cloves, peeled

freshly ground black pepper

6 or 8 pieces of toast

6 or 8 free-range eggs

Place your salt cod in a pan of clean water and bring to a boil, then reduce to a gentle simmer and cook for 14 minutes. Remove the fish from the water and allow to cool to a handleable heat. Remove any bones and skin (be warned—this is very sticky).

Meanwhile, cook your potatoes in salted water, as if for mashing. Drain when done. In two separate pans heat the milk and oil.

First whizz your garlic and a pinch of pepper in a food processor to a fine purée (as once the other ingredients are added you will never get rid of any garlic chippings). Once this is achieved add the cod and potatoes, then have the motor running and add in equal quantities, bit by bit, the hot oil and milk until you achieve the right consistency; a giving, slightly hairy purée.

As a starter, serve warm with toast and 8-minute, firmish boiled eggs. As a main course, spread thickly on toast and top with a poached egg.

FISH AND SHELLFISH

141

BRILL BAKED ON GREEN AND WHITE VEGETABLES

TO SERVE TWO TO SIX

Brill is a beautiful flat, white fish. In the fish hierarchy they are grander than plaice, not as grand as turbot or halibut, but I think the most delicious. The size of your brill will dictate the number of mouths it will feed. A medium to large brill will satisfy four to six diners, a smallish one two. It should be reasonably large so that it will withstand a cooking time long enough for the vegetables to get to know the fish juices.

You want a whole fish for this, so see what your fishmonger has; also take into account your cooking receptacles and the size of your oven.

fennel, trimmed and sliced
　　across the grain

leeks, cleaned and sliced

onions, peeled and sliced

cloves of garlic, peeled and
　　finely chopped

knobs of unsalted butter

1 large whole brill, gutted

sea salt and freshly ground
　　black pepper

1 or 2 lemons

In a pan gently sweat your vegetables and garlic in butter, just to start the softening process, but not so that they have given up all resistance. Season with salt and pepper. Lay them as a bed for your fish in your baking pan. Place the fish on its vegetable bed, dot with knobs of butter and season, then pop it into a hot 425°F oven. Check the fish with a knife—when done the flesh should part easily from the bone. Keep a very close eye after 10 minutes. Serve with lemon.

SMOKED EEL, BACON, AND MASHED POTATOES

TO FEED THREE

More of an assemblage than a recipe as such.

1 reasonably large whole smoked eel

4¼ to 4½ pounds floury potatoes, such as Idaho russets, peeled and halved

sea salt

2½ cups milk

1½ sticks (12 tablespoons) unsalted butter plus an extra knob

freshly ground black pepper

6 thick rashers (slices) of smoked streaky bacon (see page 79)

To prepare your eel, first lay it down with its back facing you. With a sharp knife cut behind its head until you feel the backbone, then run your knife along the bone to the tail. Turn over and repeat. To remove the skin simply slip your fingers under it and run gently along the fillet.

Cut both fillets into 3 pieces. (Smoked eel is also available packaged in fillets.)

Boil your potatoes until soft in salted water. Heat the milk and butter, then add to the drained potatoes and mash. Season with salt and pepper, remembering that the bacon is quite salty.

Heat a frying pan and add the knob of butter. Place your bacon slices in the pan and cook. Remove the bacon, keep it warm, and place the eel fillets in the pan, giving them a few moments' cooking on either side in the butter and the fat the bacon should have released.

Serve the eel on a mound of mashed potatoes, topped with 2 slices of bacon, over which pour the remaining bacon and eel fat from the frying pan.

FISH AND SHELLFISH

143

EEL, BACON, AND PRUNE STEW

TO SERVE EIGHT—ONCE YOU HAVE DONE BATTLE WITH THE EELS, YOU WANT TO HAVE A PARTY

You can get your eels from the fishmongers in most Chinatowns, or any good fishmonger. I recall reading somewhere someone saying that skinning an eel is like removing a lady's stocking. It is not, so leave the skin on. It will do no harm, and in fact holds the flesh together and enriches the sauce. Do, though, with a good pair of scissors, trim off the fins which run along the top and bottom of the eel. Serve with lots of white crusty bread, mashed potatoes, or white bread fried in duck fat.

1½-pound piece of smoked streaky bacon (see page 79), rind removed, rolled, and tied; bacon cut into chunks

a knob of unsalted butter

30 whole shallots, peeled

8 cloves of garlic, peeled

1 bottle of red wine

5 cups light chicken stock

a bundle of herbs, including 2 stalks of celery, tied together

2 bay leaves

14 ounces prunes (Agen if possible), with their pits in (when they have been pitted they tend to fall apart in cooking)

2 reasonable-sized eels (3 if small), cut into 1¼-inch sections

a small splash of red wine vinegar

sea salt and freshly ground black pepper

In a pot large enough to fit all your ingredients brown the bacon and its rind in butter. When the bacon has colored and has given off some of its fat, remove and keep to one side, then gently cook the shallots and garlic in the pot to a sweet golden brown. Return the bacon and rind to the pot, then add the red wine, stock, bundle of herbs, bay leaves, and prunes, and let this simmer for 15 minutes. Add the eel and cook for a further 30 minutes.

Now carefully remove all the ingredients with a slotted spoon to a bowl, discarding the herbs, and keep warm. Add your wee dash of vinegar to the sauce to counteract the sweetness of the prunes and the richness of the eel, and bring it to a boil to reduce, skimming constantly to remove any scum that may arise. This may take 10 to 15 minutes. The sauce should have a rich stickiness thanks to the eel and prunes. When happy with the juice check for seasoning and reduce the heat to a simmer. Return the other ingredients to the pot and let them warm through gently. The prunes should have swollen to delicious rich clouds. Serve.

SKATE, CAPERS, AND BREAD

If your skate wings are small serve one each, half each if largish, and cut into four pieces if large. The main thing is to make sure your fishmonger skins your wings on both sides. The white bread here does not refer to slices of stodgy, soulless, packaged bread, but a loaf with a distinguished crumb and splendid crust. You need a spirited salad to follow.

a small splash of oil per portion

1¾ sticks (14 tablespoons) unsalted butter

skate wings (see headnote), seasoned with salt and freshly ground black pepper

20 rough ½- to ¾-inch cubes of yesterday's white bread with the crusts cut off

juice of ½ lemon

a small handful of capers

a small handful of curly parsley, chopped

Heat an ovenproof frying pan that's large enough for your fish to lie flat. Apply a spot of oil and a large knob (1 to 2 tablespoons) of butter. When sizzling, pop the skate in, and *shuggle* the pan slightly to stop the flesh sticking. Turn the fish after a few moments, give the pan another *shuggle,* and place in a hot 425°F oven for about 10 minutes. Adjust for the thickness of the skate: your skate is done when the flesh comes easily from the bone when prodded with the point of a knife.

Remove the fish to a warm plate and return the pan to the heat. Add the rest of the butter, wait until this is bubbling, and add the bread cubes. Let these get a little color, and cook until crispy and buttery, but still giving in the middle. Add the lemon juice, allow it to sizzle and turn brown, and add the capers. At the last minute add the parsley and straightaway pour over the fish. Season with salt and pepper and serve at once.

VEGETABLES

PRESSED POTATOES

Let me explain first how to make this and then, once you have an idea of what I am talking about, what you can do with it. You need a loaf pan or terrine. The recipe requires a firm waxy potato; it's the starch that will act as the bonding agent in this dish.

4 pounds potatoes, such as Yukon Gold, peeled

a healthy handful of capers (extra-fine if possible)

sea salt and freshly ground black pepper

Boil the potatoes in salted water; check whether they are done with a sharp knife in order to catch them before they start to fall apart. Drain.

Line your loaf pan or terrine with plastic wrap. As soon as the potatoes are at a temperature you can handle, but still warm, slice them ½ inch thick. Lay one layer of sliced potatoes at the bottom of your chosen mould, cautiously sprinkle with capers and salt and pepper, cover this with another layer of potatoes and repeat the caper and seasoning. Continue this process until the mold is full, cover with plastic wrap, place a heavy weight (see page 51) on top (the right size to fit within the sides of the mold), and place in the refrigerator overnight.

The next day, tip the pressed potato out of its mold and slice with a thin, sharp knife.

It is a wonderful base for oily, salty things. For example, you can now dress each slice with anchovy fillets, extra-virgin olive oil, and Eel, Bacon, and Prune Stew as on page 144 . . .

MASHED PARSNIPS

Rich, sweet, and soothing.

3 pounds parsnips, peeled and
    cut in half

5 cups milk

2½ sticks (20 tablespoons)
    unsalted butter

sea salt and freshly ground
    black pepper

Boil the parsnips in the milk with a pinch of salt. When
cooked, drain them, reserving the milk. Mash with the
butter. If they seem too dry add a splash of cooking
milk. Season with salt and pepper and serve.

TURNIP BAKE

This may sound like a grim dish in a grim vegetarian café, but it is not. Unfortunately I have not been able to think up a more tempting name for this delicious dish yet. It calls out to be eaten with roast lamb.

1 onion, peeled and very thinly sliced

1¾ sticks (14 tablespoons) unsalted butter

2½ to 2¾ pounds turnips, peeled and very thinly sliced

sea salt and freshly ground black pepper

In a pan sweat the onion in 11 tablespoons of the butter until it's soft, sweet, and clear. Put to one side. Smear the remaining butter over a deep ovenproof frying pan, into which you place the first layer of sliced turnips. Add a smattering of your buttery onion mixture, season with salt and pepper, follow with another layer of turnip, and repeat this process until the frying pan is full (the turnips will shrink during cooking; do not be disappointed). Cover with aluminum foil (shiny side down; the matte side encourages the transference of heat through the foil whereas the shiny side will deflect it slightly, which at other times is just what you want). Place in a medium to hot 375°F oven for approximately 1 hour so it is thoroughly cooked. Check for a giving center with a knife. When satisfied remove from the oven, remove the foil, and allow it to calm down for about 5 minutes.

Now to serve, tip it upside down onto the appropriate-sized plate (being careful not to burn yourself in this maneuver). You should now have a brown and yielding turnip bake (it will not be crisp).

RADISHES TO ACCOMPANY DUCK OR GOOSE

TO SERVE SIX

The fresh, peppery radishes make a perfect foil for the rich birds.

3 bunches of radishes with happy leaves

juices from the roasting pan of the duck or goose, or duck fat and a splash of chicken stock

sea salt and freshly ground black pepper

Remove the leaves from the radishes and wash both the leaves and the radishes. Heat up your roasting juices or fat and stock, then add the radishes. Let this sizzle, stirring frequently. In approximately 5 minutes the radishes will have changed to pink blushing orbs, still crispy but with a hint of giving. Add the radish leaves and remove the pan from the heat. The leaves do two things: they give a wonderful flavor, and they add a structural weave, preventing your radishes from rolling all over your plate when served. Season with salt and pepper and stir, letting the leaves wilt a moment, then serve with roast duck or goose.

GREEN BEANS, SHALLOTS, GARLIC, AND ANCHOVIES

Perfect for lamb chops.

2 heads of garlic, skin on

16 shallots, peeled

extra-virgin olive oil

sea salt

12 fillets of anchovies in oil, chopped reasonably fine

a handful of capers (extra-fine if possible)

a handful of chopped curly parsley

a pinch of freshly ground black pepper

1 teaspoon red wine vinegar

2 pounds haricots verts, topped (and if you wish tailed)

Roast the garlic heads in a hot 400 to 425°F oven until they are soft when you squeeze them. Allow to cool to a handleable temperature, then squeeze the flesh out of the cloves. Toss the shallots in a little olive oil in a pan on top of the stove, then place in the oven to roast, keeping a close eye on them and tossing regularly until soft and sweet. Keep warm.

Put a pan of well-salted water on to boil. Mix the anchovies with the garlic flesh, capers, parsley, and pepper. Add a splash of extra-virgin olive oil and the vinegar.

When the water is boiling, put the beans in and boil for 4 minutes. Check whether they are to your liking, drain, then mix them in a warm bowl with the shallots and anchovy dressing.

Serve straightaway with lamb chops (which hopefully you have not forgotten to cook while doing all of the above).

ROAST TOMATOES AND CROTTINS

A *crottin*, which means horse dung or sheep's dropping in French, is a small, button-like goat cheese from France; some are for eating and others specifically for cooking with. For a while now a few American goat cheese makers have been producing them. St. John uses crottins from a goat herd in Barnet, surprisingly, so look out, there could be a crottin producer near you! The best known of these is probably Laura Chenel in California.

18 to 24 vine-ripened tomatoes (if possible, or if not, then the most delicious tomatoes available to you), depending on how large your tomatoes are

sea salt and freshly ground black pepper

20 cloves of garlic, peeled

extra-virgin olive oil

6 crottins

a large bunch of fresh mint, leaves only

juice of 1 lemon

a pile of white, long, crispy toast made by slicing the bread, drizzling with extra-virgin olive oil, and baking in the oven until golden brown at the edges and crispy

Place the tomatoes in an ovenproof dish, season with salt and pepper, scatter your garlic, and then, in a generous fashion, splash your olive oil over all. Put into a hot 425°F oven for approximately 25 minutes until the tomatoes are soft and giving. Remove from the oven and check that the garlic is soft and cooked; if not, remove the tomatoes to a plate and pop the garlic back into the oven until cooked. When ready to serve, return the tomatoes to the dish. Nestle in your crottins and return to the oven until they are giving but not gone. Once again, remove from the oven.

Slightly tear your mint leaves and dress with the lemon juice and a splash of extra-virgin olive oil. Season with salt and pepper, place in a clump on top of your tomatoes and crottins, and serve with the pile of crispy toast.

Squish the tomato, garlic, crottin, and mint onto the toast, scoop up some of the garlicky, tomatoey oil, and eat.

BAKED CELERIAC AND EGGS

A wintery lunch that is not dark brown and meaty.

1 large head of celeriac or
   2 small, peeled and cut
   into chunks

sea salt

2 sticks (16 tablespoons)
   unsalted butter,
   approximately

freshly ground black pepper

the leaves of a head of celery,
   chopped

8 free-range eggs

Place the celeriac in a pan of well-salted water, bring to a boil, and cook for approximately 25 minutes; check with a knife. When cooked, drain the celeriac: make a thorough job of this, as you do not want a watery mashed celeriac.

On a gentle heat mash the celeriac in a pan with butter, adding as much as you feel the celeriac wants to absorb. Season with salt and pepper.

Now mix the celery leaves into the celeriac. Decant this mixture into a warm ovenproof dish, and make 8 indentations in the surface of the mash, into which break 8 eggs. Season the eggs and place 2 small knobs of butter on top. Bake in a hot 425°F oven for approximately 5 minutes, keeping an eye on it, until the egg whites are firmed up, but the yolks are still runny. Serve right away.

MUSHY ZUCCHINI

In the day and age of the al dente vegetable, what a joy to find a recipe that celebrates the well-cooked, buttery vegetable.

1 stick (8 tablespoons)
  unsalted butter

4 cloves of garlic, peeled and
  very finely chopped

1 pound zucchini, topped and
  tailed, then sliced into
  rounds a little thicker than
  ⅓ inch

sea salt and freshly ground
  black pepper

In a pan on a gentle heat, melt the butter and sweat the garlic (making sure it does not brown or burn). Add the zucchini, season carefully with salt and pepper, and toss to coat with the garlicky butter. Cover and continue the gentle cooking, stirring occasionally. After 15 minutes, uncover. When some of the zucchini slices start to break, binding the whole together, check the seasoning, and serve.

ROAST PUMPKIN

What is vital here is the pumpkin. It must be an organic blue pumpkin (Hubbard) or Jarrahdale—a pale blue-skinned, very hard-fleshed, delicious pumpkin, which can be obtained at health-food shops. Once you have tried one, the large, orange, woolly variety will become a thing of the past in your life. Use a good, firm, tight pumpkin or squash, not those that are stringy or fluffy. Butternut squash is a good substitute if you can't find a blue pumpkin.

As to the roasting, simply cut it in half, scoop out the seeds, then cut into ¾-inch moon crescents. Place the pieces on a baking pan skin side down, drizzle with extra-virgin olive oil, season with salt and pepper, and roast in a hot 400°F oven, basting occasionally. This should take 20 to 25 minutes. Check with a knife to see when it's soft.

Be careful not to overcook your pumpkin, as it will dry out.

DRESSINGS, SAUCES, AND PICKLES

VINAIGRETTE

TO MAKE APPROXIMATELY 1⅓ CUPS

You can do this in the food processor or by hand.

2 cloves of garlic, peeled

1½ generous teaspoons Dijon mustard

a pinch of sea salt and freshly ground black pepper

juice of 1 lemon

1 generous teaspoon white wine vinegar

1¼ cups extra-virgin olive oil

Crush your garlic (making sure this is finely done, as you don't want chips of garlic in your dressing), add the mustard, salt and pepper, lemon juice, and vinegar, then, as you mix, slowly add the olive oil so you get an emulsion. Once all the oil is added check the dressing for taste; you can add more salt and pepper, lemon juice, or vinegar at this point.

The lemon juice and vinegar used together seem to set each other off, avoiding a too-bitter lemon result, and the juice tempers the vinegar rather in the same magical way whiskey and lemon juice meet in a whiskey sour, both becoming something else altogether. This keeps very well in the fridge.

DRESSINGS, SAUCES, AND PICKLES

AÏOLI

Aïoli often seems to be mistaken for a garlic mayonnaise, but this is not so. Aïoli is aïoli and eating it should be an emotional experience—it is strong, but that is its role in life. Purists would disagree, but I find a food processor very useful here; the final consistency seems to hold together better. The instructions assume you will, too, but if you prefer there is always the mortar and pestle. Of course, if you don't have a food processor, all you need to remember is mash your garlic well and add your oil gently. Purists may also disagree about the inclusion of eggs. Sorry.

20 cloves of garlic, peeled

sea salt and freshly ground black pepper

2 free-range egg yolks

about 2½ cups extra-virgin olive oil

juice of 2 lemons (you may not need all the juice but it is best to have it at hand)

Put the garlic in a food processor with a pinch of salt (this helps to break it up) and pepper. Whizz until finely pulped (this is important, as you do not want garlic chippings in the aïoli). Add the egg yolks, let them meet the garlic for a moment, then carefully and slowly add the oil in a gentle stream. The emulsion should safely hold up to 2 cups oil; at this point take a view and, if you can, add a little more oil. Now add the lemon juice, tasting as you go, adjust the seasoning, then refrigerate. A couple of hours let the aïoli find its feet.

MAYONNAISE

You can use a food processor, or a mortar and pestle, or a bowl and wooden spoon. Some use vegetable oil rather than olive oil for a gentler result. I do not. Your mayonnaise should have that bitter olive taste. Some thin with water; I feel this should be avoided.

3 free-range egg yolks

1 generous teaspoon Dijon mustard

sea salt

about 2½ cups extra-virgin olive oil

a healthy splash of lemon juice

a healthy splash of white wine vinegar

freshly ground black pepper

Place the egg yolks, mustard, and a gesture of salt in a food processor, and mix, then drizzle oil in very slowly, especially at the beginning so as to achieve an emulsified mixture. You can add up to 2½ cups oil; if you feel confident that the emulsion will hold, add more oil. If it is getting too thick add a splash of lemon juice and white wine vinegar; you can always add more oil. Season with salt.

After a while you will learn the various noises mayonnaise makes in the making that tell you when you have enough oil. These are hard to describe in words so I'm afraid you just have to listen to it. You want a consistency that has a body to it, but a body with give, not one that goes *boing* when you put a spoon in it.

If you are using a mortar and pestle, or bowl and spoon, follow the same process, but I stress the importance of the most gentle of drizzling of oil with this method.

DRESSINGS, SAUCES, AND PICKLES

163

GREEN SAUCE AND ITS POSSIBILITIES

PLENTY FOR SIX

Green sauce is a wonderful thing and goes with almost every meat, roast, boiled, or cold; vegetables; and some fish. Its companions know no bounds. The parsleys are essential, the other herbs good additions—rejig the parsley if you're not including any of them. Never use a food processor to make Green Sauce, as you will end up with a pulp rather than a textural delight.

half a bunch of curly parsley, leaves only

half a bunch of flat-leaf parsley, leaves only

half a bunch of mint, leaves only

a quarter-bunch of dill, leaves only

a small showing of tarragon leaves (it has a habit of taking over if added in too-large quantities)

1 small can of anchovy fillets, finely chopped

12 cloves of garlic, peeled and finely chopped

a handful of capers, roughly chopped (if extra-fine keep whole)

extra-virgin olive oil

crushed black pepper

Finely chop your herbs, but not too finely, and mix with the anchovies, garlic, and capers. Add olive oil to reach a loose, still spoonable, but not runny or oily, consistency. Taste and season with black pepper (the anchovies should negate any necessity for salt).

Its possibilities

There are many things you can add to this sauce: chopped cornichons (but do this just before serving, as they tends to discolor the sauce if left standing), and chopped egg are two of the finest.

Depending on how coarsely you chop your herbs, even if at all, it can become more of a salad than a sauce. Or, on the other hand, it makes a splendid salad dressing when diluted by the addition of more oil or vinaigrette.

You have five wonderful things:

Capers

Anchovies

Extra-virgin olive oil

Garlic

Parsley

There is no end to the possibilities . . .

TOMATO KETCHUP

You will need a stainless-steel pan, large enough for all the ingredients. Tie the peppercorns, allspice, and cloves in cheesecloth. This ketchup will improve with age.

7¾ pounds tomatoes, roughly chopped

2 pounds apples, peeled, cored, and chopped

6 onions, peeled and chopped

4 cups sugar

1 quart malt vinegar

2 tablespoons sea salt

1 teaspoon cayenne pepper

12 black peppercorns

12 whole allspice

12 cloves

Place all the ingredients in a stainless-steel pan, bring to a boil, and reduce to a simmer; you want to cook until the ingredients are a pulp, which should take approximately 2 hours. Remove from the heat and press through a sieve. Return the resulting mixture to the pan and heat to reunite it after its pressing experience. Boil for 2 or 3 minutes and then decant into sterilized jars and seal. Allow it a few days to find its feet, and then it is ready to use in all its many ways.

HORSERADISH SAUCE

A very fine thing.

5-inch piece of fresh
   horseradish, peeled

juice of ½ lemon

1¼ cups crème fraîche

sea salt and freshly ground
   black pepper

Finely grate the horseradish. This can be quite an emotional experience and may bring tears to your eyes, but is very good for clearing the sinuses. Sprinkle the grated horseradish with lemon juice to prevent its discoloring. Mix gently with the crème fraîche and season to taste.

It's ready.

ANCHOVY DRESSING

A food processor or a mortar and pestle is important for this recipe.

7 cloves of garlic, peeled

a pinch of freshly ground
black pepper

1 small can anchovies in oil

scant 1⅓ cups extra-virgin
olive oil

a splash of red wine vinegar

Place the garlic and pepper in the food processor or mortar and crush to a fine purée, then add the anchovies and allow them to break down. Start to add the oil, then the vinegar to taste. Check the flavor for seasoning.

This dressing, depending on how thick you make it, can have many uses.

With less oil and vinegar added you will have a very firm mix that is delicious spread on toast and eaten with sweet roasted shallots. If the full amount of oil and vinegar is added you should have a looser, though still emulsified mixture, which is ideal for dressing boiled greens or broccoli (which can be eaten on their own or are excellent with lamb or beef), or it makes excellent dressing for raw bitter salad leaves.

TARTAR SAUCE

I realize this is old hat, but there are so many strange versions of this classic sauce served that I feel it is justified for me to add my recipe to the fray.

1⅓ cups Mayonnaise of a firmish nature (page 163)

a handful of capers (extra-fine if possible)—make sure these are well drained

a handful of cornichons, chopped in a coarse fashion, not into round or long sections

2 hard-boiled free-range eggs, peeled and chopped neither too fine nor too coarse

3 sprigs of tarragon, leaves only, chopped

a small handful of curly parsley, chopped

Mix all the ingredients together and serve.

MINT SAUCE

Another classic sauce, which has been chronicled many a time; I recently made it and found it so good, I cannot resist mentioning it. The ingredients should expand experientially to achieve your chosen movement in the sauce.

1 teaspoon Demerara sugar

2 teaspoons malt vinegar (keep it near at hand in case a splash more is needed)

1 teaspoon boiling water

a bunch of mint, leaves picked from the stems and finely chopped

Melt the Demerara sugar into the vinegar, with the aid of the boiling water. Pour over the mint and mix. If you feel it is too dry, or not sharp enough, adjust with a little more malt vinegar.

MUSTARD DRESSING FOR GREENS

TO MAKE JUST UNDER 1 CUP

This simple dressing just gives a lift to greens and is perfect with pork sausages, bath chaps (page 80), or brined and smoked pork chops. It keeps well in the fridge.

3 teaspoons Dijon mustard

1 teaspoon red wine vinegar

⅔ extra-virgin olive oil

sea salt and freshly ground
   black pepper

Mix the ingredients together and toss your boiled greens in the mixture. Serve immediately so that the greens do not cool down.

ST. JOHN CHUTNEY

There is nothing finer, after having a good stock up your sleeve, than having a reserve of chutney.

3 pounds apples, peeled, cored, and chopped

2 pounds shallots, peeled

10 cloves of garlic, peeled

3 pounds tomatoes, chopped

2 pounds dates

2 pounds raisins

scant ½ pound fresh ginger, peeled and coarsely grated

2 pounds dark brown sugar, or to taste

2½ cups malt vinegar

TIED TOGETHER IN CHEESECLOTH

black peppercorns

whole coriander seeds

white peppercorns

whole chiles

allspice

mace

bay leaf

celery seeds

cloves

fennel seeds

mustard seeds

Take a large stainless-steel pot with a thick bottom that won't be affected by the vinegar, and bring all the ingredients together. Cook on a gentle heat, stirring occasionally to avoid sticking at the bottom, for approximately 1 hour. What you want is a brown chutney look and consistency—this may take some more cooking, but be careful not to go too far: you do not want to end up with a brown, jammy consistency. When satisfied, remove the spice bag and bottle in clean, sealable sterilized jars. Keep in the fridge for at least 2 weeks before eating.

GREEN BEAN CHUTNEY

This recipe comes from Joan Chapman, who has won many a prize with her chutneys and vegetables at the Great Bedwyn Village Fête, so we are in very capable hands. Runner beans are long, flattish green beans, often sliced on the diagonal. The more you pick them, the more there seem to be the next day.

2 pounds runner beans, trimmed and cut diagonally into ½-inch lengths

sea salt for the water, plus 1½ teaspoons

1½ pounds shallots, peeled and chopped

2¼ cups malt vinegar

1½ pounds Demerara sugar

1 teaspoon Coleman's Dry English Mustard Powder

1½ tablespoons ground turmeric

2 tablespoons cornstarch

Cook the beans for 5 minutes in salted water and drain. Cook the shallots in half the vinegar for 10 minutes, then add everything except the cornstarch and the remaining vinegar and cook slowly for approximately 30 minutes. Mix the cornstarch with the remaining vinegar, add, and cook for a further 10 minutes, stirring constantly. Decant into clean, sterilized sealable jars and keep for a few weeks, if you can, before eating.

PICKLED SHALLOTS

A version of the pickled onion that makes lively company for meats hot or cold, and cheese. Use small round shallots, peeled but left whole.

2 pounds shallots, peeled but
    left whole

1 pound coarse sea salt

malt vinegar

white wine vinegar

8 cloves

10 allspice

2 whole cinnamon sticks

8 white peppercorns

10 black peppercorns

4 bay leaves

12 coriander seeds

4 small dried hot chiles

Cover the shallots with brine (made with the salt and 7 cups water) and leave to soak in a plastic, glass, or china container for a week in the fridge.

Now you know how much liquid it takes to cover your shallots; heat the same amount of a mixture of half and half malt vinegar and white wine vinegar in a stainless-steel pan with the collection of spices. While this comes up to a simmer, rinse the shallots thoroughly and then place in the simmering spiced vinegar for 5 minutes. Remove from the heat and bottle in clean, sterilized sealable jars and keep for a month somewhere cool. They are now ready to use. The leftover spiced vinegar is very good for dipping cooked whelks in. In France they are called *bouleau*; they look like sea snails.

PICKLED GHERKINS

An incredibly useful thing to have up your sleeve. After many failures in the restaurant at pickling gherkins, I was shown the way by Anna Rottman, a friend of my wife's from New Zealand.

¾ cup coarse sea salt

4¼ to 4½ pounds gherkins

pickling spice (you can buy this already mixed), which should include celery seed, mustard seed, black peppercorns, small dried red chile, coriander seed, and dill seed

4 cups sugar

3 tablespoons acetic acid

5 cups water

Wash your gherkins, sprinkle them with salt, and leave to stand for 2 to 3 hours, occasionally tossing them gently. Shake off the salt and place the gherkins in a bowl, cover with clean boiling water, and leave them to stand for 5 minutes. Drain.

Place the gherkins in clean, sterile, sealable jars, adding a healthy, many-fingered pinch of pickling spice to each jar. Meanwhile, place the sugar, acid, and water in a stainless-steel pan and boil until the sugar and acid have dissolved. Pour hot over the gherkins.

Seal the jars while the liquor is still hot. Keep in your cupboard for at least a month before eating.

PUDDINGS

AND

SAVORIES

TREACLE TART

The extraordinary thing is that however full you're feeling, when it comes to treacle tart you can always manage to find space for it. Don't worry about the extra pastry, better to have extra. This pastry is very delicate and you will need to allow a day to make the tart.

Hot or cold, it wants to be eaten with thick cream.

PASTRY

1½ sticks plus 2 tablespoons unsalted butter

¼ cup plus 2 tablespoons sugar

1 free-range egg, beaten with a fork

¾ cup ground almonds

1¾ cups all-purpose flour

FILLING

6 cups fresh white breadcrumbs

1½ cups Lyle's Golden Syrup

grated zest and juice of 2 lemons

First cream the butter and sugar together until they are light and fluffy, then add the eggs, gradually mixing as you go to avoid curdling. Fold into this mixture your almonds and flour. Now a light touch is vital—not too much, but enough; the less you mix or handle your pastry the better.

This will produce a very soft pastry, so rest it in the fridge for a good 8 hours. You may have problems rolling it out, so resort to pressing it into the tart pan with your thumb: remember to aim for a thin tart shell. If time is on your side, allow this to rest in the fridge for 1 hour then bake blind (unfilled) in a medium to hot 375°F oven for 15 minutes, watching closely to make sure it doesn't burn.

Mix the filling ingredients together, fill the blind-baked shell, and bake in a medium to hot 375°F oven for 40 to 45 minutes. When ready remove from the oven and allow to sit for 10 to 15 minutes, serving it warm to allow it to restructure itself. The top should be firm; it looks like a rough but tempting golden desert (sic). It is also wonderful cold or at room temperature.

BAKED TREACLE PUDDING

The Golden Syrup can be replaced by jam with equally joyous results. A pudding basin is a kind of china bowl that goes into the oven.

7 tablespoon unsalted butter, softened, plus 2 small knobs

½ cup superfine (caster) sugar

2 free-range eggs

¾ cup self-rising flour

grated zest of 1 lemon

a pinch of sea salt

6 tablespoons Lyle's Golden Syrup (I was advised 4 tablespoons by those in the know, but that is simply not enough)

To start, take one of your knobs of butter and grease a 2-cup pudding basin. For the sponge mixture, cream the 7 tablespoons butter and sugar with a spoon, then add one of the eggs. Mix the egg in gently with 1 rounded teaspoon of your flour, to prevent the mixture from curdling, then follow with the other egg. Once the eggs, butter, and sugar are one, add the lemon zest and fold in the rest of the flour and the salt.

Pour your Golden Syrup (or jam) into the pudding basin and then put the sponge mixture on top of this. Cover the basin with buttered aluminum foil (use butter knob number two), including a tuck allowing for the expansion of the sponge, then bake in a medium to hot 375°F oven for 35 to 40 minutes. It is done when you can stick a skewer in and pull it out clean.

When its cooked, turn it out onto a warmed dish deep enough for the escaping Golden Syrup (do not worry, this will work). Serve straightaway with lots of cream at hand.

GOAT CURD AND MARC

Goat curd is available, but if you can't find it, a log of young goat cheese, before it has formed a rind, will suffice.

2 tablespoons superfine (caster) sugar

2 large shots of marc de bourgogne (you can reduce the marc content if you find it too heady)

1½ pounds goat curd

Stir the sugar into the marc until it has all melted (you do not have to apply heat for this), then mix into the goat curd.

Eat with plain sweet cookies and/or red fruit.

ST. JOHN'S ECCLES CAKES

SHOULD EASILY MAKE A DOZEN CAKES—IF YOU HAVE PASTRY LEFT OVER IT FREEZES VERY WELL

I stress the *St. John* in our Eccles cake, as I am sure Eccles cake bakers in Eccles will not recognize them as an Eccles cake they know.

Oddly enough, for a restaurant with a certain carnivorous reputation, we serve a vegetarian Eccles cake, omitting to use the traditional lard in the pastry; instead we use puff pastry, so apologies to Eccles, but this recipe's results are delicious and particularly fine when consumed with Lancashire cheese, a fresh, sharp, and crumbly cheese.

Eccles cakes take their name from the town of Eccles. It is a small flaky cake containing currants, but one of those dishes that much debate arises from, almost to the same extent as the discussion of what should go into a proper cassoulet. But the rigor of the Eccles cake discussion is that there are far fewer elements to disagree on, hence I stress Lancashire cheese, whose fresh, sharp qualities are the perfect foil for the rich currant filling.

PASTRY

- 9 tablespoons unsalted butter, plus 3 sticks plus 3 tablespoons unsalted butter, both cold from the fridge
- 4 cups unbleached flour
- a pinch of sea salt

FILLING

- 4 tablespoons unsalted butter
- ½ cup plus 1 tablespoon packed dark brown sugar
- 1½ cups currants
- 1 teaspoon ground allspice
- 1 teaspoon ground nutmeg

GLAZE

- 3 egg whites, beaten with a fork
- a shallow bowl of superfine (caster) sugar

To make the puff pastry

Mix the 9 tablespoons butter with the flour and salt using your fingers until the mixture resembles breadcrumbs, then cautiously add 1 cup water and mix until you have a firm paste. Pat into a square and wrap in plastic wrap. Leave to rest in the fridge for at least 1 hour before using.

Once it's rested, roll the paste into a rectangle about ⅜ inch thick; between sheets of wax paper, beat the 3 sticks plus 3 tablespoons butter into a rectangle a wee bit smaller than half the paste rectangle. Lay the butter rectangle on the paste, leaving a space at the end. Fold the unbuttered half over the butter and crimp the edges, so you now have butter in a paste package. Pat into a square, wrap in plastic wrap, and allow to rest in the fridge for at least 15 minutes. Roll out into a rectangle in the opposite direction to your initial major fold—each time you roll out the pastry to fold, turn your pastry and roll across the previous direction you rolled. (You will have to sprinkle flour on the surface of your rolling pin; it is very important to dust the flour off the paste before folding it at every turn in the process.) Once the pastry is about ½ inch thick, fold like a traditional letter, with one end of the rectangle to the halfway mark, and the other end over this. Pat square and place in the fridge for at least 15 minutes to rest again. Repeat this process two more times, but no more! This is essential for a successful puff. Return to the fridge and rest for 1 hour or more. Do not be deterred; in writing this seems like a more complicated process than it is in practice.

To make the filling

Melt the butter and sugar together, then add them to the currants, allspice, and nutmeg, mix well, and then leave to cool before using.

To make the Eccles cakes

Roll the puff pastry out to a ⅜-inch thickness and cut circles approximately 3½ inches in diameter. On half of these spoon a blob of your filling mixture in the center of the circle, then place the other pastry circles on top. Pinch the edges together, gently press to flatten the cakes, then slash the top three times (I'm told it is very significant how many times an Eccles cake is slashed). Paint the top with egg white, then dip it into the sugar. The cakes are now ready to bake for 15 to 20 minutes in a medium to hot 400°F oven; keep an eye on them so that they don't burn. They can be eaten hot or cold and are particularly marvelous with Lancashire cheese.

CHOCOLATE ICE CREAM

With the aid of Leah White, my pastry chef (who has been a great help with various puddings and pastries and their technicalities), we tried to create a wonderful dark bitter chocolate ice cream. We have failed so far, so if anybody can help, please communicate with us at St. John at 011 44 20 7251 0848. Even so, seeing as chocolate ice cream is fundamental, I have included the recipe we currently use. It is not as dark or as bitter as I could wish for, but is rich and delicious.

I'm afraid before you go any further you will need an ice-cream machine.

⅔ cup milk

1½ cups 40% heavy cream

2 ounces chocolate of 70% cocoa solids, roughly chopped

5 free-range egg yolks, ready in a bowl

⅝ cup superfine (caster) sugar, ready in another bowl

2 ounces of unsweetened chocolate, roughly chopped

Put the milk and cream into a pan, bring it up to a boil, reduce to a gentle simmer, and add the 70% solids chocolate. Now add the egg yolks to the sugar and beat well. When thoroughly beaten add a little of the hot cream mix, whisking quickly. This mixture is now added to the cream and milk in the pan on the stove. Stirring lively as you go, let this cook for 8 to 10 minutes. Continue stirring, but not so lively, and add the unsweetened chocolate. Allow this to melt. Once that has happened, pass the whole lot through a fine sieve. Allow it to cool slightly before placing it in your ice-cream machine, then churn and freeze in a clean container.

It should be ready in a couple of hours, or will keep for another day, but a word of warning: do not keep it for too long, as homemade ice cream is better eaten freshly made.

CARRAGHEEN PUDDING

Carragheen is a small red seaweed with great setting properties, found in the Hebrides and Ireland. If you're not in either of these places picking from the shore, there's a good chance your local health-food shop will have it—or, bring it back dried from holidays in Ireland and Scotland.

½ pound carragheen

5 cups milk

3 to 4 tablespoons superfine (caster) sugar or to taste

thick heavy or clotted cream and good jam to accompany

Put the carragheen, milk, and sugar into a pan, and bring to a gentle simmer, stirring occasionally, for about 20 minutes, by which time the carragheen will appear to have half melted. Strain the liquid, discarding the remains of the seaweed, into a bowl and put in the fridge to set. It should turn out with ease.

This may sound like a very dour milk pudding, but let me assure you the carragheen gives the dish many particular qualities, some of which are hard to put one's finger on.

In its purity it goes very well with very thick, rich cream and a blob of good jam.

TOM'S CHERRY TRIFLE

For this recipe I leave you in the capable hands of Tom, a man of many talents who has served St. John's well, in and out of the kitchen!

The individual recipe components should ideally be made the day before the pudding is to be served. Also, this trifle doesn't really work when done as one large bowlful because, unlike my mother's, the fruit isn't set in a jelly but in a thick compote and so remains a little runny.

THE CUSTARD

1¼ cups milk

1¼ cups 40% heavy cream

1 vanilla bean, split lengthwise and scraped

4 free-range egg yolks

½ cup plus 1 tablespoon superfine (caster) sugar

THE TRIFLE SPONGES

6 free-range eggs, separated

1¾ cups superfine (caster) sugar

1¼ cups all-purpose flour

¼ cup cornstarch

confectioners' sugar for dusting

THE CHERRY COMPOTE

2 tablespoon superfine (caster) sugar

1 pound black cherries, washed and pitted

juice of ½ lemon

The custard

Place the milk, cream, and vanilla pod in a saucepan and bring to a boil. In a large round-bottomed bowl whisk the yolks with the sugar until smooth.

When the milk and cream have come to a boil pour them onto the yolks and whisk until thoroughly blended. Return to the pan and stir with a wooden spoon. Cook over a gentle heat until the custard coats the back of the spoon. Whatever you do, do not let the custard boil or it will curdle and be unusable. Pass through a fine sieve and set aside to cool.

The trifle sponges

Place the yolks in a mixing bowl and add half the sugar. Whisk by hand or with an electric mixer until light and fluffy. In a separate clean bowl whisk the whites until they form soft peaks, then, as you continue to whisk, slowly add the remaining sugar. Sift together the flour and cornstarch. Cover a baking sheet with a Silpat mat or parchment paper.

Now begin folding the mixtures together. Fold one third of the egg whites and one third of the flour into the yolks and repeat until all the mixtures are combined.

You can either pipe the mixture onto the baking sheet in traditional finger shapes or (much easier) spread it evenly

sherry or Marsala for soaking

crème fraîche or clotted
    cream for serving

toasted almonds for serving

on the sheet. Either way dust the mix with confectioners' sugar and place in a warm to medium 325°F oven for approximately 15 minutes, but keep a close eye on it. When lightly golden remove from the oven and leave to cool. This recipe is more than ample but the sponge keeps for weeks if stored in an airtight tin.

The cherry compote
Place the sugar in a small stainless-steel pan, and dissolve it with a little water, making sure that the sides of the pan are clean and free of sugar crystals. Place over a gentle heat. Boil until it thickens to a dense, uncolored syrup: if you have a candy thermometer it's the soft ball stage; if you haven't look for a glucose consistency with large bubbles. When it reaches this point throw in ¼ pound of the cherries and the lemon juice and stir well. Turn down the heat and let the cherries stew for 10 minutes.

Carefully pour the mixture into a blender and purée. While hot pour the mixture onto the remaining fruit, cover, and leave to steep and soften. When all your ingredients are cool you can begin to assemble the trifle.

Assembling the trifle
Divide the cherry mixture among the 6 ramekins but do not fill any more than one-third full. Next place a layer of diced trifle sponge and soak with medium-dry sherry or, if you feel a little extravagant, Marsala, and allow to seep in for 10 minutes or so. Press down and pour the custard over, ideally leaving a little space at the top of the ramekin.

Place in the fridge overnight but remove 30 minutes before it is to be served. To finish, spoon over some crème fraîche or, to be utterly sinful, a dollop of clotted cream, and a sprinkling of toasted almonds.

WELSH RAREBIT

a knob of unsalted butter

1 tablespoon flour

1 teaspoon Coleman's Dry
English Mustard Powder

½ teaspoon cayenne pepper

1 cup Guinness stout

a very long splash of
Worcestershire sauce

1 pound mature strong
Cheddar cheese, grated

6 pieces of toast

Melt the butter in a pan, stir in the flour, and let this cook together until it smells biscuity but is not browning. Add the mustard and cayenne, stir in the Guinness and Worcestershire sauce, then gently melt in the cheese. When it's all of one consistency remove from the heat, pour out into a shallow container, and allow to set. Spread on toast ½ inch thick and place under the broiler. Eat when bubbling golden brown. This makes a splendid savory at the end of your meal, washed down with a glass of port, or a steadying snack.

SAVORIES are a particularly British way to end a meal, obviously not something sweet, a dish more appropriately washed down with a glass of port. For example, Welsh Rarebit, Soft Roes on Toast (page 133) or, historically, Bone Marrow were often eaten as a savory.

BAKING

THE STARTER

Here are some bready pearls of wisdom passed on to me, and now to you, by Manuel Monade, baker. This is stage one in the baking process, a way of improving the flavor and texture of your crumb, and establishing the amount of yeast you need to use. So a little forward thinking—this needs to be prepared the day before you make your actual dough (of which this is an element) for your bread.

1 quart water, blood warm
   (about 98.6°F)

14 cups bread flour

a tiny pinch of fresh yeast
   (dry yeast can be used if
   fresh is unavailable)

Mix the ingredients together thoroughly with your hands and place in a clean bowl or plastic container. Cover and store in the fridge for a day before using.

Your starter will keep for a week in the fridge.

WHITE BREAD

Do not attempt too large a loaf if you have any doubt about your oven's capabilities.

1 pound starter (see page 189)

¼ ounce fresh yeast

1⅔ cups water, blood warm (about 98.6°F)

3½ cups bread flour, plus extra for dusting

a pinch of rye flour

2 tablespoons fine sea salt

Mix all the ingredients, except the salt, together thoroughly in a bowl using your hands. At the final moment of mixing add the salt. Dust a flat clean surface with flour, tip the mixture out of the bowl, and knead it for approximately 5 minutes—not aggressively, do not fight with your dough, but gently and purposefully. This is important to remember all the way through handling the dough. Now place in a clean bowl, cover it with plastic wrap, and put to rise in a warm place (not hot, just warm) for 45 minutes.

Dust your work surface with flour again. Now scoop and tip the swollen dough onto the surface. Knead for another 5 minutes. Shape into loaves, place on a floured baking sheet, cover loosely with plastic wrap, and return to your warm spot for a further 45 minutes. Halfway through this rising, give the loaves a gentle stretch in the direction of your chosen shape.

Place a baking sheet into a hot 425°F oven and allow this to become very hot, then place your loaves on the sheet. Bake for between 20 and 30 minutes; 10 minutes into the baking time spray the loaves in the oven with water (use one of those things you spray plants with), which will improve the crust. To learn whether the bread is ready, turn the loaf over and tap its bottom: if it sounds hollow like a drum it's ready.

When you are happy with your bread, remove the loaves from the oven and allow them to cool on a rack.

BROWN BREAD

½ pound starter
(see page 189)

⅓ ounces fresh yeast

2¼ cups water, blood warm
(about 98.6°F)

3½ cups bread flour

1¼ cups rye
flour

1¼ cups

whole wheat flour

2 tablespoons fine sea salt

The procedure is the same as for the white bread recipe, page 190.

CRACKERS

Excellent crackers to eat with cheese.

6½ cups plus 2 tablespoons
  bread flour

2 teaspoons baking powder

1 teaspoon poppy seeds

1 teaspoon dill seeds

1 teaspoon caraway seeds

2 teaspoons sea salt

¾ cup extra-virgin olive oil

about 1⅔ cups cold water

Sift the flour and baking powder together, then mix in the poppy, dill, and caraway seeds, and the salt. Stir in the olive oil, then cautiously add the water: you want a fairly soft dough, but not sticky. The dough is now ready to use.

On a large flat surface sprinkle some flour and dust your rolling pin. Roll out the dough to a thickness of approximately ¼ inch, then cut into your chosen shape. May I suggest a round with 2-inch diameter? The dough left can be kneaded together and rolled out again. Roll the cut shapes out again as thin as you can, place on a clean baking sheet, then put in a medium to hot 375°F oven, and bake for 10 minutes, keeping a close eye on them so as to avoid burning (don't worry if you do burn them, you are not alone: somehow fate has it that one burns crackers, so bake them in batches).

Allow to cool on a rack. Eat or store in an airtight container.

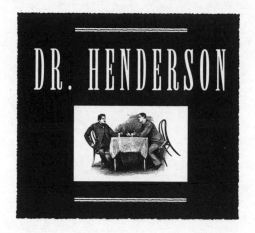

DR. HENDERSON

A MIRACLE

Here is a cure for any overindulgence, taught to me by my wise father.

2 parts Fernet Branca
1 part crème de menthe
ice

Mix together and drink. Do not be put off by the color.

Be careful: this is so effective you can find yourself turning to its miraculous powers with increasing regularity. Do not let the cure become the cause.

INDEX